The information provided in this book is for informational and training purposes only and is not intended to be a source of advice with respect to the material presented. In addition, the author has made every effort to ensure that the information in this book was correct at the time of release and whilst this publication is designed to provide accurate information in regard to the subject matter covered, the author assumes no responsibility for errors, inaccuracies, omissions, or any other inconsistencies herein. This publication is meant as a source of valuable information for the reader, however it is not intended as a substitute for direct professional advice. The use of this book implies your acceptance of this disclaimer.

# Table of Contents

## Acknowledgements

I am deeply grateful to Corrie Leitch for her unwavering support and encouragement.

To those professionals who kindly agreed to be interviewed, thank you for your time and expertise.

My heartfelt thanks goes to my cousin Natalie Tomlinson, for her patience and guidance in proofreading and copy editing this book to get to the final result.

# Preface

When I first considered writing this book, I was determined to make it interesting, engaging, perhaps even humorous in parts. But I quickly admitted defeat and the truth of it – risk management and insurance is and always will be a dry subject. To try and make it anything but that would negate its purpose – to ensure safety for people and protection of assets.

Having been in insurance for over 20 years, I have found myself drawn to the construction industry. Why it fascinates me, I do not know. Having gained a wealth of knowledge on the topic, and a long established love of writing, I decided to write this guide. Aimed at new underwriters, brokers, and other insurance professionals, it may not be a fun and exciting read, but I hope it is found to be easy to read, informative, and as interesting as is possible.

This does not provide everything there is to know about the construction industry, but it is a good start for anyone who finds the topic quite daunting - a response I have often seen throughout my career. I do not profess to be an expert in the subject, but I do feel I can help people with grasping the basics.

The guide only covers Liabilities and Contractors' All Risks perspectives, but there are other aspects to consider that I feel I do not know enough about to guide you, although some aspects are touched upon as they overlap with the areas I focus on. Professional Indemnity, Directors & Officers, Legal Expenses including Contract Disputes are some such areas.

I realise that not everyone has the same interest in the topic as me, but I hope you find it useful. I have included some interviews with trade professionals - an underwriter, a broker and a contractor - which I hope will provide some interesting real world perspectives.

The idea behind this book is to provide some much needed training material to the insurance industry, so that the construction industry is a much less daunting sector for those just starting out in commercial insurance.

# Construction Terminology

The construction industry involves more than just bricks and mortar. Many people feel overwhelmed when they encounter a labyrinth of terminologies and concepts.

So let's have a look at some technical terms, to gain a clear understanding of their significance in the construction realm, with the main emphasis being on terms used in construction projects that are key to insurance considerations.

## Employers Liability: Guarding the Workforce

The well-being of the workforce stands as a paramount concern within the construction industry. Employers Liability encapsulates the legal and ethical responsibility of safeguarding workers' interests. This involves creating a safe work environment, offering training, and providing adequate protection against any harm that may arise in the course of their employment, including injuries and illnesses.

## Public Liability: Safeguarding the Public Domain

Construction projects often exceed the confines of the worksite and interact with public areas. Public Liability underscores the importance of ensuring that construction activities don't inadvertently cause harm to third parties or their property. It is the accountability for preventing accidents or damage that could affect people or property outside of a construction space.

## Construction - what do we mean?

This refers to the various activities, processes, and efforts involved in the creation, alteration, repair, or demolition of physical structures or infrastructures. It encompasses a broad range of tasks, from the planning and design stages to the actual building or modification of structures, such as buildings, roads, bridges, and other facilities. Construction can vary widely in scale and complexity, ranging from small residential projects to large-scale infrastructure development. It can require coordination among various professionals, including architects, engineers, contractors, and subcontractors, to ensure that the project is completed successfully and in accordance with design specifications and safety standards.

Key elements:

- Planning and design: The initial phase involves architectural and engineering planning, where the design of the structure is conceptualised and detailed plans are created.
- Site preparation: This includes clearing the land, excavating, and making the site ready for construction.
- Foundation work: The construction of the base or foundation, which provides stability and support for the entire structure.
- Structural construction: The assembly of the main framework or structure of the building or infrastructure, involving walls, floors, roofs, and other essential elements.
- Installation of systems: This includes the incorporation of essential systems such as electrical, plumbing, HVAC (heating, ventilation, and air conditioning), and other utilities.
- Finishing work: The final touches, including interior and exterior finishes, painting, flooring, and other aesthetic elements.
- Landscaping: If applicable, landscaping work to enhance the surroundings of the constructed structure.

- Demolition and removal: In cases of renovation or replacement, the demolition and removal of existing structures.

Whilst a construction project can be a multi-million pound contract that involves numerous different parties, and can be carried out over a duration measured in years, there is also the other end of the scale, where a self employed plumber, electrician, or roofer could be undertaking repair work at a residential property. These types of contracts are short but large in quantity, and still pose hazards that must be considered.

## First Fix and Second Fix

There are two building stages that are referred to as first fix and second fix. First fix is more about structural and service installation; second fix is about finishing and detailing.

First fix refers to the initial phase of construction work where the basic structure of the building is established. This includes all the work that needs to be completed before the internal finishes are applied. The first fix involves the installation of structural elements and the preliminary installation of essential services. The goal of the first fix is to establish the core infrastructure of the building, ensuring all necessary systems are in place before proceeding to finishing work. The components are:

- Structural Framework: Erecting walls, floors, and roof structures.
- Initial Plumbing: Installing pipes for water supply, waste, and drainage systems.
- Electrical Wiring: Laying cables and wiring for electrical systems.
- HVAC Systems: Initial installation of heating, ventilation, and air conditioning ductwork.

- Window and Door Frames: Fitting the frames, though not the actual windows and doors.

Second fix refers to the phase of construction that involves the completion of the building's interior and exterior finishes. This includes all the work that comes after the basic structure and preliminary services have been installed. The goal of the second fix is to complete the building's interior and exterior to a finished standard, ready for occupation. The components are:

- Plumbing Fixtures: Installing sinks, toilets, baths, and other plumbing fixtures.
- Electrical Fittings: Installing light switches, sockets, and lighting fixtures.
- Carpentry: Fitting skirting boards, architraves, doors, and kitchen units.
- Decorative Finishes: Painting, tiling, and flooring.
- Final HVAC Components: Installing radiators, thermostats, and final ductwork adjustments.

The main hazards in first fix include structural hazards, electrical risks and plumbing Issues. During second fix, the main hazards are tool use, chemical exposure, and slips and trips.

## Certificate of Completion

A Certificate of Completion is an official document issued upon the successful completion of a construction project or a specific phase of the project. This certificate signifies that the work has been finished according to the agreed-upon specifications, standards, and contractual requirements. It marks the end of the contractor's obligations under the contract and can trigger final payments, release of retention monies, and the start of maintenance/warranty periods during which the contractor may be responsible for addressing defects or issues that arise.

A thorough inspection is carried out to ensure all aspects of the project meet the required standards and specifications before the certificate is granted.

## Different Types of Contractor

The classification of contractors into different types often relates to the nature of their relationship with the entity or organisation for which they are performing work. Here are explanations of the common types of contractors: direct employees, labour only subcontractors, and bona fide subcontractors.

Direct employees are individuals who work directly for an organisation or employer. They are typically hired through a formal employment process, receive regular wages or salaries, and are subject to the employer's control and direction.

Characteristics:

- Employees have a direct contractual relationship with the employer.
- They are subject to the employer's supervision and management.
- Wages are often paid on a regular basis, and the employer is responsible for deducting taxes and providing benefits.
- They require cover under both EL and PL.

Labour only subcontractors are individuals or firms that provide specific labour services to a primary contractor. They are engaged by the contractor to perform specific tasks or services, usually related to manual or skilled labour.

Characteristics:

- The subcontractor provides labour services but not materials or equipment.
- They work under the direction and control of the primary contractor.

- Payment is often based on the amount of labour or work completed rather than a fixed salary or wage.
- For the purposes of insurance, they are treated the same as employees and require cover for both EL and PL under the companies insurance policy.

Bona fide subcontractors are independent entities or individuals hired by a primary contractor to perform a specific part or aspect of a larger project. Unlike labour only subcontractors, bona fide subcontractors are generally responsible for providing their own materials, equipment, and expertise to complete the designated portion of the work.

Characteristics:

- Bona fide subcontractors operate as independent businesses or entities.
- They have their own contracts with the primary contractor.
- Subcontractors are responsible for their own insurance, and liabilities, however there is still a contingent liability for the main contractor as they are responsible for the overall contract, so they need to be factored into the PL cover of the main contractor (normally a percentage less than 50% of the main employee rate).
- Documentation of appropriate cover and risk assessments are to be provided to the main contractor.
- They may have more autonomy in managing their work, schedule, and resources – they may be supervised by the main contractor, or they may work independently.

## Contract Works: Protecting the Materials

This relates to everything that is used in the course of the contract - the materials themselves such as concrete blocks and glazing, and equipment such as scaffolding and temporary buildings. This can also be referred to as the 'works' and this term will be used throughout the book.

## Materials, Equipment, and their Common Uses

Concrete - Foundations, slabs, columns, and various structural elements.

Steel - Structural framing, reinforcement in concrete, and various building components.

Brick and masonry - Walls, facades, and partitions.

Wood - Framing, flooring, doors, and finishes.

Asphalt - Roads, pavements, and roofing.

Glass - Windows, doors, and facades.

Plastics - Pipes, insulation, and decorative elements.

Insulation Materials - Insulating walls, roofs, and floors for energy efficiency.

Scaffolding - Providing access to elevated areas for tasks like painting or installing components.

## Temporary Works

This refers to structures, equipment, or installations erected on-site for the sole purpose of facilitating construction activities, but are not for incorporation within the project itself. These temporary structures are essential for supporting the construction process, ensuring safety, and enabling the completion of the project. Temporary works encompass a wide range of temporary structures, including scaffolding (which can also be classed as own plant or hired in plant), formwork, falsework, shoring, temporary access platforms, temporary excavations and support systems.

Contract Works insurance policies typically provide coverage for temporary works as part of the overall project coverage, and is usually defined under 'Contract Works'.

## Temporary Buildings

This refers to structures erected on-site for temporary use during construction projects. These structures may include site offices, storage facilities, welfare facilities, or temporary accommodation for workers.

Temporary buildings provide essential amenities and facilities to support construction activities, such as administrative offices, equipment storage, restrooms, break areas, and first aid stations. They are typically erected at the beginning of a construction project and remain in place until project completion or until they are no longer needed. Temporary buildings are generally defined and covered as Hired In Plant or Own Plant.

It is key to note that temporary buildings primarily serve as functional spaces for administrative, storage, or welfare purposes, while temporary works are designed to support and facilitate construction activities directly.

## Plant and CPA Conditions

Own plant refers to the machinery, equipment, and tools owned by a contractor or construction company. These are the assets used in the construction process, such as excavators, cranes, concrete mixers, and other specialised tools.

Hired in plant, also known as hired plant or hired equipment, refers to machinery, equipment, or tools that a contractor or construction company rents or hires from another party for use on a specific project or a specified period. Terms of use, insurance responsibilities, and other conditions are usually outlined in a hire agreement, the most common of these being CPA conditions. These conditions are a set of standardised terms and conditions used in the hiring of plant and equipment within the construction industry. They are developed and regulated by the Construction Plant-hire Association (CPA) to ensure fairness, clarity, and consistency in plant hire agreements between equipment suppliers (hire companies) and users (hirers). These Conditions outline the contractual terms and obligations of both parties involved in the hire agreement, covering the use, operation, maintenance and return of the hired equipment. They provide established guidelines for equipment inspection, testing, and acceptance upon delivery, as well as procedures for reporting defects, damages, or breakdowns during the hire period, all to uphold operational efficiency and minimise risks during use. They will specify the duration of the hire period, rental rates, payment terms, and any additional charges or fees associated with the hire, and outline procedures for terminating or extending the hire agreement, including notice periods, termination fees, and conditions for early termination or cancellation.

The Conditions will incorporate safety and compliance standards to ensure that the hired equipment meets regulatory requirements, industry standards, and manufacturer specifications.

Importantly, they will specify whether the hire company or the hirer is responsible for arranging insurance coverage for the equipment during the hire period and may stipulate insurance requirements, including minimum levels of insurance coverage, indemnity clauses, and liability limits.

They will also provide mechanisms for resolving disputes, disagreements, or breaches of contract between the hire company and the hirer.

As these Conditions are a recognised industry standard, they are preferred by insurance companies for their clarity, consistency and transparency, however non-standard Conditions are considered if provided to insurers for review, ensuring there is no unexpected liability aspects that would be picked up under the agreement.

**Plant and their Common Uses**

Excavators - Excavating foundations, trenches, and grading.

Cranes - Lifting steel beams, concrete elements, and other heavy components.

Concrete mixers - Preparing concrete for foundations, slabs, and structural elements.

Bulldozers - Clearing land, grading, and site preparation.

Dump trucks - Hauling materials to and from construction sites.

Power tools - Drills, saws, and grinders for cutting, shaping, and fastening materials.

Welding equipment - Connecting steel components in structural elements.

Whilst company tools would be classed as own plant, there are also employees tools. These tend to be less specialist, complex or valuable.

## Contract Works Terminology

**Project Documentation**

All projects are based on contract conditions, and the larger and more complex the project, the same applies to the contract and other documentation.

There are three main documents that are produced by contractors that are of particular interest to insurers when considering cover for individual, large contracts:

A *site plan* is a detailed drawing or map that depicts the layout, features, and dimensions of a construction site. It provides a comprehensive overview of the site's physical characteristics, including placement of existing structures, roads and parking areas, utilities, topography, access points and boundaries, and other infrastructure elements on the construction site.

It provides accurate measurements and dimensions of various site features to facilitate construction planning and coordination, as well as depicting existing site conditions, such as terrain, vegetation, soil types, and environmental factors, influencing construction activities.

It identifies the location of underground utilities, including water lines, sewerage systems, electrical cables, and gas lines, to avoid accidental damage during construction.

Whilst site plans provide valuable information for contractors, engineers, architects, and other project stakeholders to understand site constraints, optimise space utilisation, etc., it also assists insurers in considering the size and the estimated maximum loss – the more spread out the works is, the less likely it will be that there is a total loss.

A *Gantt chart* is a visual project management tool that illustrates the scheduled timeline of project tasks, activities, and milestones over a specified period. It consists of horizontal bars representing individual tasks, arranged chronologically along a time axis. The key components are:

- Enumerates all project tasks, activities, and deliverables required for project completion.
- Specifies the estimated duration or duration range for each task, expressed in days, weeks, or months.
- Indicates the logical relationships and dependencies between tasks, such as task sequences, predecessors, and successors.
- Highlights significant project milestones, key deliverables, or critical events that mark project progress or completion points.
- Allocates resources, such as labour, equipment, and materials, to specific tasks based on project requirements and availability.

Gantt charts provide a visual representation of project schedules, allowing project managers and team members to track progress, identify bottlenecks, and manage project timelines effectively. They facilitate communication and coordination among project stakeholders by providing a clear overview of project activities, deadlines, and dependencies.

Gantt charts enable project managers to adjust schedules, allocate resources, and resolve conflicts to ensure timely project delivery and meet client expectations.

They are also extremely helpful to insurers – having details of all the activities and their duration will give them an understanding of the complexity of the contract, any high risk activities to consider, and if the contract is very large, then the ability to build a rate based on the breakdown of activities and their duration.

A *Schedule of Works*, also known as a work schedule or project timeline, is a detailed plan that outlines the sequence, duration, and resources required to complete individual tasks, activities, and phases of a construction project.

The key components are:

- Describes the scope of work, objectives, and specifications for each project task or activity.
- Specifies the planned start and finish dates for each task, reflecting the scheduled timeline for project execution.
- Identifies the resources needed to complete each task, including labour, equipment, materials, and subcontractors.
- Assigns responsibility for task execution and oversight to project team members, subcontractors, or external stakeholders.
- Provides mechanisms for tracking and reporting progress, including milestones, checkpoints, and performance indicators.

Schedule of works facilitates project planning, scheduling, and monitoring, enabling project managers to identify potential delays, allocate resources efficiently, and implement corrective actions to keep the project on track.

For insurers, it is another tool to fully understand the contract in detail and the hazards involved.

**Phased Handovers**

A phased handover refers to the sequential transfer of completed portions or stages of a construction project from the contractor to the client or end-user over multiple phases or stages. Instead of handing over the entire project upon its completion, the handover occurs incrementally, allowing the client to gain access to and begin utilising specific areas or components of the project as they are completed. Here's a breakdown of the process and its significance:

- Identification of phases - The project team identifies distinct phases or stages of the construction project based on project requirements, construction sequencing, and client needs.
- Completion of phases - Construction activities are executed in accordance with the project schedule, with each phase completed incrementally. As individual phases reach substantial completion, they undergo quality checks, inspections, and final preparations for handover.
- Client acceptance - Once a phase is deemed substantially complete and meets the agreed-upon quality standards, the client or end-user conducts an inspection and formally accepts the completed portion of the project.
- Handover process - Formal handover procedures are conducted for each phase, involving documentation, certification, and transfer of responsibility from the

contractor to the client. This may include turnover of keys, operation manuals, as-built drawings, warranties, and other relevant project documentation.

- Occupancy and utilisation - Following the handover of each phase, the client gains access to and begins occupying or utilising the completed areas for their intended purpose. This allows for early occupancy, fit-out works, and operational preparations while construction continues on remaining phases.

- Continuation of construction - Construction activities progress simultaneously across multiple phases, with subsequent phases entering construction or completion stages as earlier phases are handed over. This ensures a seamless transition and continuous advancement of the project toward overall completion.

The benefits of a phased handover for contractors include - in addition to operational and revenue benefits - a reduction of project risks by allowing early identification and resolution of issues, defects, or discrepancies in completed phases before they impact subsequent construction stages.

From an insurance perspective, phased handovers on larger projects are preferred - this reduces the exposure at risk, as it is no longer the contractors responsibility (other than the maintenance period where they are responsible for any defects identified from their works).

## Estimated Original Contract Price

The estimated original contract price represents the anticipated total cost of completing a construction project, identified prior to the start of a contract. This normally includes a contingency allowance to account for unforeseen events, changes in scope, or project uncertainties. It serves as a buffer to cover unexpected expenses and mitigate the risk of cost overruns during construction. It serves as a fundamental factor in determining the coverage limits and premiums of an insurance policy. Further details of how this ties in with insurance coverage can be found under the Policy Cover and Exclusions section.

Remember that these definitions provide a basic understanding of each term. Insurance policies will vary based on specific circumstances. It's always advisable to consult with professionals in the relevant fields to obtain accurate and comprehensive information.

# What are the General Liability Concerns on a Contract Site?

As you can imagine, a construction site can be a complex and hazardous environment, which is why safety precautions and protocols are of utmost importance. For the purposes of this book, a contract site can be anything from a huge construction site for the new build of a school, to the kitchen of a residential flat where a plumber is fixing or installing the pipes under a sink.

First of all, let's take a look at one of the main hazards on a contract site, from both a liability and a contract works perspective: Fire. From inception hazards to fire loads, there are numerous considerations on site that can pose significant risks to workers, property, and the surrounding environment.

*Hot work*: Activities such as welding, cutting, soldering, and grinding generate sparks and heat, which can ignite nearby flammable materials, including construction debris, insulation, or combustible gases.

*Electrical systems*: Faulty or overloaded electrical systems, temporary wiring, and improperly installed electrical equipment can lead to electrical fires. Damaged extension cords, exposed wiring, and overloaded circuits are common causes of electrical fires on contract sites.

*Combustible materials*: Construction materials, such as wood, insulation, paint, solvents, adhesives, and fuel containers, are highly flammable and can ignite easily if not stored or handled properly.

*Smoking:* Smoking on construction sites poses a fire hazard, especially when workers improperly dispose of cigarette butts or smoking materials near combustible materials or flammable liquids.

*Flammable liquids and gases*: Storage and handling of flammable liquids, such as gasoline, diesel, propane, and paint thinners, require proper ventilation, containment, and safety measures to prevent accidental spills, leaks, or ignition sources.

*Equipment and machinery*: Overheating equipment, engines, and machinery can ignite nearby materials or fuel sources. Combustible materials accumulating near hot surfaces or exhaust systems pose additional fire risks.

*Open flames*: Open flames from temporary heating devices, torches, or cooking equipment can ignite nearby materials if not monitored closely or placed in designated areas away from combustible materials.

*Arson and vandalism*: Deliberate acts of arson or vandalism on construction sites can result in significant property damage, loss of materials, and disruptions to project timelines.

Let's have a look at some of the other key liability concerns on a contract site:

**Worker safety**: The well-being of workers is paramount. Construction sites involve heavy machinery, power tools, scaffolding, and various other potential hazards. Other contract sites may be hazardous in other ways, such as working at height or with hazardous substances. Employers have a responsibility to provide proper training, safety equipment, and a safe working environment to minimise the risk of accidents and injuries.

**Third-party safety**: Contract sites often interact with the public and neighbouring properties. Any accident or injury that occurs to third parties due to construction activities can lead to liability claims against the construction company or property owner.

**Defective materials or design**: Liability may arise from the use of faulty or substandard construction materials, or if the design of the structure is flawed. In such cases, architects, engineers, and suppliers could be held responsible.

***Contractual obligations***: Many construction projects involve multiple parties, such as contractors, subcontractors, and suppliers. Liability issues may arise if any party fails to meet its contractual obligations, leading to project delays, financial losses, or accidents.

***Environmental impact:*** Construction activities can affect the environment, causing soil erosion, pollution, or damage to natural habitats. Failure to comply with environmental regulations can result in legal repercussions and liability.

***Compliance with Regulations***: Construction companies must adhere to a myriad of regulations. Failure to comply with these laws can result in fines, project delays, and potential legal problems.

***Negligence and accidents:*** Accidents can still happen despite taking necessary precautions. In such cases, determining fault and liability becomes crucial. Negligence on the part of a worker, supervisor, or company can lead to liability claims.

Now let's delve into the first point in more detail; worker safety. There are numerous hazards to consider when trying to ensure a safe working environment:

***Manual handling and lifting:*** Components can be heavy and cumbersome to handle. Improper lifting techniques or inadequate equipment can lead to musculoskeletal injuries for workers.

***Struck-by and caught-between hazards:*** Workers can be struck by falling steel or timber, tools, or other materials if not properly secured. They may also get caught between moving or collapsing elements.

***Electricity:*** Construction sites often have electrical tools and equipment. Workers must be cautious about electrical hazards, such as electrocution or electrical fires.

***Tool and equipment accidents:*** The use of power tools and equipment during construction can lead to injuries if not used correctly or if proper safety measures are not followed.

***Weather-related risks:*** Construction workers are exposed to outdoor elements, which can include extreme heat, cold, rain, or wind, leading to heatstroke, hypothermia, or other weather-related illnesses, as well as weather-related accidents.

***Structural collapse:*** During the erection of structural frames, improper construction techniques or inadequate bracing can lead to structural failures and collapses.

***Inadequate training and supervision:*** Workers who are not adequately trained or supervised might not be aware of safety protocols, leading to an increased risk of accidents.

**Efficacy**

In the context of this book, efficacy, or 'failure to perform' refers to the effectiveness or performance of the work or services provided by a contractor. Specifically, it addresses whether the contractor's actions and outcomes meet the intended purpose, function and expectation of the contract. The concept of efficacy is significant in the insurance industry, particularly when assessing the potential risks and liabilities associated with the work performed by contractors.

Key points include:

Contractual obligations - Efficacy is tied to the contractor's ability to fulfil their contractual obligations. It assesses whether the work performed aligns with the agreed-upon specifications and meets the standards set forth in the contract.

Liability considerations - The efficacy of a contractor's work is closely linked to liability considerations. If the work is found to be ineffective or if it results in damage, injury, or financial loss, the contractor may be held liable, and insurance coverage may come into play.

Scope of coverage - Insurance policies may explicitly address the efficacy of work in their terms and conditions. Contractors and businesses should carefully review their insurance policies to understand the scope of coverage related to the effectiveness of their services. There are some trades that are considered higher risk and insurance policies may specifically exclude efficacy. One such trade is electrical contractors, and we will look at efficacy in more detail under that section.

Contractors are encouraged to implement quality assurance and risk management practices to enhance the efficacy of their work. This proactive approach can contribute to minimising the likelihood of errors, defects, or performance issues that could lead to insurance claims.

# What other Concerns are there on a Contract Site?

Let's explore some other concerns that lurk amidst the dust and debris.

## Property Damage

This is an ever-present worry on contract sites. Mishaps with heavy machinery, tools, or even accidental fires can lead to costly damage to neighbouring properties or existing structures. This would be a higher risk where there are existing structures. Going back to the new build of a school versus plumbing in a flat – the former would have nothing but a metaphorical blank slate to work from, a cleared site and no existing structure at risk, but the latter involves the risk of damage to the occupants' belongings, and those of neighbouring flats, adjacent or below.

*Flood risk*: Construction sites are vulnerable to weather elements – Rainfall, flash floods, or inadequate drainage systems can wreak havoc, causing delays, erosion, and damage to construction progress. Improper site selection can exacerbate flood risks, also resulting in erosion and construction delays. Proper water management strategies and contingency plans are necessary to address flood-related concerns.

*Theft of materials*: Valuable construction materials, such as lumber, steel, copper piping and equipment such as tools and plant, can be subject to theft, leading to project delays and financial losses.

*Plant theft*: From excavators to bulldozers, these vital assets can be targeted by unscrupulous individuals, leading to frustrating setbacks. Plant theft can significantly disrupt construction progress and increase project costs.

Some other factors to consider include:

**Traffic Management**

There are various features of traffic management to consider, both at the entrance to a construction site, and within the boundary of it. Particularly on larger sites where there will be numerous different contractors on site at once, and others who may be entering or leaving the site at the same time, it is important to consider the following features:

What is the access to the site like -

- Is it a single track road?
- Does it allow the passage of multiple vehicles - is it quite a wide open area?
- Is there restricted access with clearly visible signs for the general public to stay clear?
- Is there clear and defined boundary lines/appropriate fencing?

How is the site entrance managed -

- Are there supervisery staff there in high-visability workwear, and/or temporary traffic lights present?
- Is there clear signage/guidance for the contractors in how they should operate/enter the site?

All of this will build a picture of how the risk is minimised in respect of impact (from vehicle movement in and out of the site) and injuries (caused by moving vehicles).

**Project Delays**

These can have a significant impact on the costs involved and the length of time a contract takes to complete, resulting in a knock on effect on future or coinciding contracts. Fully understanding the project, the materials needed, and the specialist knowledge/experience needed to carry out the work will indicate where potential issues may lie.

At the design and planning stage, there should be detailed information on every single aspect of the project - procurement, resource allocation, and workflow sequencing. There will always be potential for design changes due to client requests, regulatory requirements, or unforeseen conditions, but expected/predictable factors should be planned for as much as possible.

Weather conditions within the UK have a massive impact on projects, and can delay them by up to 21%. Where contracts are being undertaken in the depths of winter or height of summer, planning for adverse conditions and temperatures is imperative. Working at height, on roofs, or the use of cranes can all be affected, as well as the welfare and health of contractors, are just some of the aspects of construction work that can be impacted by weather conditions.

Adverse weather conditions are expected to be factored into project planning and should be addressed within the contract. Where contracts are silent on weather conditions, they will be the responsibility of the contractor. JCT standard contracts state that the Employer is responsible for delays due to weather conditions, however 'exceptionally adverse weather conditions' are not defined. The JCT work with the Met Office to provide two weather report forms that assist with project management and planning. When adverse weather conditions affect a project, there is often need for an extension of time (EOT) to complete the work. However, the interpretation and allocation of EOTs can become a grey area and may lead to disputes between project stakeholders. Contracts typically include provisions for granting EOTs due to adverse weather. However, the specific criteria for granting EOTs, the duration of delays considered reasonable, and the responsibility for mitigating weather-related impacts can vary, leading to interpretation disputes.

Establishing the extent of weather-related delays and their impact on project schedules requires accurate documentation and evidence, including weather data, site conditions, and productivity records. Inconsistencies or gaps in documentation can complicate dispute resolution.

Weather-related delays can result in additional costs, such as extended labour, equipment rentals, and overhead expenses. Disagreements over who bears the financial burden of weather-related delays can escalate into disputes over contract terms and compensation.

In order to mitigate the risk and additional costs associated with weather-related project delays, there are a number of strategies that can be used.

Utilisation of technology: Advanced weather forecasting technologies and data analytics tools enable construction teams to anticipate weather events more accurately and plan work schedules accordingly. Real-time weather monitoring and predictive analytics help mitigate the impact of adverse weather on project timelines.

Historical data analysis: Analysis of historical weather data for the project site provides valuable insights into seasonal weather patterns, extreme weather events, and their potential impact on construction schedules. This information helps project teams proactively plan for weather-related risks and allocate resources more effectively.

Contractual clarity: Clear and detailed contract provisions regarding weather-related delays, EOTs, and dispute resolution mechanisms help minimise ambiguity and prevent disputes. Contracts should clearly define the criteria for granting EOTs, the documentation required, and the process for resolving disputes related to weather delays.

Regular project meetings and transparent communication channels facilitate the identify of weather-related risks, proactive risk management and dispute resolution.

Other possible project delay reasons include the following, which can be sufficiently be prepared for by stringent planning, ensuring adequate supplies are available and regular equipment inspection:

Material shortages - whether due to supply chain disruptions, transportation issues, or procurement challenges.

Labour shortages - Shortages of skilled labour, subcontractor availability, or workforce disruptions, such as strikes or labor disputes.

Permitting and approvals - Delays in obtaining necessary permits, approvals, or regulatory clearances from local authorities or government agencies.

Unforeseen site conditions - Such as soil instability, environmental contamination, or underground utilities.

Equipment breakdowns - Mechanical failures or breakdowns of construction equipment, machinery, or tools

Subcontractor issues - Delays or disruptions caused by subcontractors, such as scheduling conflicts, quality issues, or financial problems.

Contractual disputes - Disputes or disagreements between project stakeholders, including clients, contractors, subcontractors, and suppliers, over contract terms, payment issues, or project changes.

Effective project management, proactive risk management, clear communication, and contingency planning are essential for mitigating and addressing potential causes of project delays on construction sites.

**Distance from the Nearest Whole-Time Fire Brigade**

This is to be checked and recorded as part of the project planning, and there will be communication between the contractor and the fire brigade to ensure appropriate safety and evacuation procedures are in place. For larger contracts, or those classed as high risk, there must be a fire marshal and deputy fire marshal present at all times throughout the project.

# Timber Frame Construction

Let us look in a bit more detail at some non-standard construction methods - starting with timber frame - to understand what they are, why they are used and the hazards linked to them.

## What is Timber Frame Construction?

Timber frame construction is a traditional building method that utilises large, solid wood beams and posts to create the primary structural framework of a building. This construction technique has been used for centuries and is renowned for its durability, aesthetic appeal, and sustainable qualities. However the quality of the wood used in the modern era is generally not considered as durable as the wood used up to the start of the twentieth century. In the past, joinery was carried out using slow grown oak, while nowadays it has to be grown as quickly and economically as possible due to housing requirements.

In timber frame construction, skilled craftsmen join wooden beams and posts using intricate woodworking techniques such as mortise and tenon joints, dovetails, and lap joints. These joints provide a secure and stable connection, allowing the structure to support the weight of the building without the need for load-bearing walls.

The versatility of wood is a significant advantage of timber frame construction. Various types of wood can be used, each offering unique properties such as strength, resistance to decay, and visual appeal. Commonly used woods include oak, pine, fir, cedar, and spruce.

One of the key benefits of timber frame construction is its sustainability. In an era where environmental consciousness is paramount, timber frame construction is favoured. Wood is a renewable resource, and responsible forestry practices ensure the replanting of trees, making it an environmentally friendly building material. Additionally, timber has natural insulating properties, which can contribute to energy efficiency in the built environment. Timber frame construction allows for spacious and open interior layouts, as the large wooden beams provide structural support, eliminating the need for numerous interior walls.

While timber frame construction is deeply rooted in tradition, ingenious engineering and contemporary innovations have breathed new life into this timeless method. Incorporating timber with steel connectors, reinforced with shear panels, and adorned with energy-efficient windows and insulation, modern timber frame buildings offer the perfect blend of heritage and efficiency. It continues to be a popular choice for various building types, from residential homes and barns to commercial structures and public buildings. There are numerous benefits of this construction method, which is particularly popular in Scotland for residential buildings.

Some of the considered benefits of timber frame across the UK, and particularly in Scotland, where this method is utilised heavily include:

*Abundance of timber resources:* The UK boasts extensive forests with a rich variety of timber species, including spruce, pine, and oak. This abundant supply of wood makes timber frame construction a natural choice, as it allows for the use of locally sourced and sustainable building materials.

*Traditional building technique:* Timber frame construction has a deep-rooted history in Scotland. Many historic buildings in the country, including castles, churches, and traditional homes, were constructed using timber frames. This historical legacy has influenced the continued preference for timber frame construction in both restoration projects and new buildings.

*Aesthetic appeal:* Scotland's landscapes are renowned for their natural beauty, making timber frame structures an attractive choice for both rural and urban settings.

*Energy efficiency:* The natural insulating properties of wood contribute to energy efficiency in buildings. The UK's colder climate makes energy-efficient construction methods highly desirable, and timber frame buildings can provide superior thermal performance, reducing heating costs and environmental impact.

*Construction speed:* Timber frame construction is often faster than traditional masonry methods. The UK's changeable weather conditions can be challenging for construction projects, and timber frame construction offers a quicker construction process, minimising exposure to the elements.

*Sustainable building practices:* The UK places a strong emphasis on sustainable construction practices and environmental conservation. Timber frame construction aligns well with these values, as it utilises renewable resources and has a lower carbon footprint compared to other building materials.

*Building Regulations and standards:* There are specific building regulations and standards that promote energy efficiency and sustainable construction. Timber frame construction often meets or exceeds these requirements, making it a popular choice for developers and homeowners seeking compliance with these regulations.

*Architectural flexibility:* Timber frame construction allows for design flexibility, making it suitable for a wide range of architectural styles and building types. This adaptability appeals to architects and builders who seek to create unique and innovative structures.

**What Concerns are there with Timber Frame Construction?**
This type of construction is a traditional technique with many
advantages, but like any construction method, it also comes with
certain hazards, including:

*Fire risk:* Timber is a combustible material, so if not treated with
fire-resistant coatings or adequately protected from fire sources, it
can pose a significant fire hazard. There would only be 5-10
minutes to put out a fire during construction of a timber frame
construction before the whole structure was lost, as well as any
other similar structures within 10 metres.

*Structural integrity:* If the timber used is of poor quality or not
properly treated for durability, it can lead to compromised
structural integrity over time. This could result in sagging floors,
leaning walls, or even collapse.

*Moisture and rot:* Exposure to water or moisture without proper
protection can cause timber to decay and rot, weakening the
structure and potentially leading to safety issues. Storage
considerations are needed to ensure there is no exposure to water
damage prior to its treatment and use.

*Pest infestations:* Insects like termites can infest and damage
untreated timber, leading to structural damage and instability.

*Shrinkage and settling:* Timber has a natural tendency to shrink or
settle over time, which could cause gaps, cracks, or unevenness in
the building's structure.

*Connections and fasteners:* Inadequate or improperly installed
connections and fasteners can lead to weak joints and
compromised structural stability.

*Insufficient wind resistance:* Timber frame buildings require
proper engineering and design to ensure they can withstand high
winds.

*Construction delays:* Timber frame construction can be sensitive
to weather conditions, and delays in construction can lead to

prolonged exposure to the elements, potentially causing material damage.

*Building code compliance:* Specific building codes and regulations may require additional fire protection measures, structural engineering, or treatments to address timber frame construction hazards adequately.

Let's look into the last point in more detail. In the UK, building regulations serve as a set of guidelines and requirements that must be adhered to during the design and construction of buildings. These regulations are overseen by the government and local authorities to safeguard the well-being of occupants, protect the environment, and maintain construction standards at a high level. Timber frame construction, with all its charm, also has specific regulatory considerations to ensure it is safe and resilient.

One essential aspect of timber frame construction revolves around fire safety. As we all know, timber is a combustible material and it is highly susceptible to fire . To tackle this, the Fire Protection Association (FPA) steps in. This expert body, specialising in fire safety, provides valuable guidance and recommendations to address fire hazards associated with timber frame buildings.

In compliance with the building regulations, timber frame structures undergo rigorous fire testing and assessments to meet strict safety standards. These tests evaluate the fire resistance of various timber elements, ensuring they can withstand fire for an adequate duration, allowing occupants enough time to evacuate safely.

As timber frame construction gains popularity for its eco-friendliness and energy efficiency, the government and related bodies keep a close eye on its sustainability practices. Sustainable timber sourcing is encouraged, promoting responsible forestry management and reducing environmental impact.

It's worth noting that building regulations are not set in stone and are continuously evolving to keep up with advancements in construction practices and materials. This ensures that timber frame buildings can embrace innovation while maintaining their safety and integrity.

Construction professionals, architects, and builders must stay informed and up-to-date. The regulations may vary depending on the region and project specifics, making careful attention to detail a must.

# Modern Methods of Construction

Modern Methods of Construction (MMC) refer to innovative and efficient construction techniques that have emerged to meet the evolving needs of the construction industry. These methods leverage advanced technology, prefabrication, and off-site manufacturing to streamline the building process and deliver high-quality structures with improved efficiency. MMC encompasses a diverse range of approaches, some of which include:

*Prefabrication:* This involves manufacturing building components, such as walls, floors, and roof trusses, in a controlled factory environment. These prefabricated elements are then transported to the construction site and assembled, reducing on-site labour and construction time.

*Modular construction:* Modular construction involves creating entire sections or modules of a building in a factory setting. These modules are then transported to the site and assembled like building blocks, allowing for rapid construction and minimised site disruptions.

*Volumetric construction:* Volumetric construction is a form of modular construction where entire rooms or living spaces are prefabricated as individual units. These volumetric modules are later assembled on-site to form complete buildings.

*Panelised construction:* In this method, building components are manufactured as panels in a factory, including walls, floors, and roofs. These panels are then delivered to the construction site and assembled to create the final structure.

*3D printing:* Additive manufacturing, or 3D printing, is being explored as a cutting-edge MMC technique. It enables the creation of intricate building components using computer-controlled printers, providing new possibilities for design and customisation.

***Light gauge steel framing:*** Light gauge steel framing involves using lightweight steel components to create the building's framework. This method is popular for its strength-to-weight ratio and suitability for both residential and commercial projects.

***Tunnelform methods:*** Widely used for building repetitive cellular structures such as residential apartments, hotels, student accommodations, and prison cells. This method integrates both formwork and scaffolding systems to create a seamless and efficient process for casting concrete walls and slabs. Tunnelform enables the simultaneous casting of walls and slabs in a single operation. The technique uses a large, reusable steel formwork that forms both the walls and the ceiling slab of a structure. Ideal for projects with repetitive layouts, this method enhances efficiency and speed of construction by allowing daily cycle times for casting concrete sections. It is cost effective, provides high quality finishes with accurate dimensions, and produces monolithic structures with structural integrity. The disadvantages include high initial costs, limited flexibility and requires careful planning and logistics, as well as skilled labour and technical expertise to set up and operate the system correctly.

***Green construction:*** While not a specific technique, green construction principles and sustainable practices are integral to modern methods of construction. These methods focus on using environmentally friendly materials and energy-efficient designs to reduce the building's environmental impact.

Some of the more recent innovative materials include the following:

***Osmotic cement:*** Also known as self-healing or bio-cement, this is a type of cement that possesses the ability to repair cracks and damage autonomously through a process similar to biological healing mechanisms. It contains special additives or microorganisms that react with water or other substances present in the environment to form minerals that fill in cracks and gaps, restoring the material's integrity. Osmotic cement has the potential to be used in a variety of construction applications, including concrete structures, bridges, tunnels, and roads, where durability and resilience to damage are critical. Benefits can include prolonging the lifespan of concrete structures, reducing maintenance costs, and improving sustainability by minimising the need for repairs and replacements.

*Translucent concrete:* Also known as light-transmitting concrete or transparent concrete, it is a composite material that allows light to pass through it while retaining its structural integrity. Translucent concrete is typically made by embedding optical fibers or other light-transmitting materials within a matrix of traditional concrete. It can be used in architectural applications such as façades, interior walls, pavements, and decorative elements, where designers seek to incorporate natural light or create visually stunning effects. Translucent concrete offers unique aesthetic possibilities, allowing architects and designers to create spaces that are both visually striking and functional. It can enhance natural lighting, reduce energy consumption, and create dynamic visual effects.

*Engineered timber:* Also known as mass timber or engineered wood, it refers to wood products that are manufactured by bonding together smaller wood components to create larger, stronger, and more durable structural elements. Engineered timber products include cross-laminated timber (CLT), glued laminated timber (glulam), and laminated veneer lumber (LVL), among others. As an example, CLT is a sustainable building material made from layers of solid wood boards, stacked crosswise and glued together. It offers structural strength and design versatility, promoting timber-based construction methods. Engineered timber is increasingly being used in a wide range of construction applications, including residential, commercial, and institutional buildings, as well as bridges, pavilions, and other structures. It offers several advantages over traditional building materials, including sustainability, cost-effectiveness, design flexibility, and faster construction times. It also has excellent structural performance, fire resistance, and thermal insulation properties. The adoption of modern methods of construction is driven by various benefits, including reduced construction time, enhanced quality control, improved safety, and minimised waste. These innovative approaches pave the way for a more efficient and sustainable construction industry, shaping the buildings of the future while addressing contemporary challenges of the present.

## MMC and Fabric First Approach

MMC is an increasingly used method of construction, as contractors are encouraged to use the 'fabric first' construction approach. The initiative is one which aims to promote low carbon emissions, energy efficiency, and sustainability from the design stage, with these important factors being taken into account from this stage to post-construction. Materials, machinery and plant, and techniques that are used must focus on this result. A completed building must be sustainable and energy efficient. More traditional construction materials, such as brick or stone, have higher production and transport costs, and buildings take longer to construct. This all means that they have a higher carbon emission and lower energy efficiency compared to the MMC materials.

## What about the Risks of using MMC?

MMC may bring numerous advantages to the construction industry, but they also introduce specific hazards and liability concerns that require careful consideration. Let's explore some of the potential hazards from different perspectives:

**Liability Concerns:**

- Quality and workmanship: With off-site manufacturing and assembly, the risk of errors or defects in the prefabricated components increases. If substandard materials or workmanship are present, it can lead to safety issues and potential liability claims.
- Design errors: The design phase of MMC requires precision and thoroughness. Any design flaws or omissions can result in construction errors or safety hazards, exposing stakeholders to liability risks.
- Transportation and installation: Transporting and handling large prefabricated components poses challenges. Accidents during transportation or improper installation on-site can lead to accidents, injuries, and property damage, potentially leading to liability claims against the responsible parties.
- Third-party relationships: MMC often involves multiple contractors, subcontractors, and suppliers. Miscommunications or delays between parties can result in contractual disputes and potential liability issues.

**Contract Works Concerns:**

- Supply chain disruptions: MMC relies heavily on the timely delivery of prefabricated components. Delays in the supply chain can cause interruptions in the construction schedule and lead to issues.
- Coordination and assembly: Integrating various prefabricated elements on-site requires efficient coordination. If there are inconsistencies in the components or delays in assembly, it can affect project timelines and costs.

- Compliance and approval: Meeting regulatory requirements and obtaining necessary approvals for innovative MMC techniques may cause delays and affect project progress.
- Durability and damage: The materials incorporated within the works, such as polystyrene or recycled materials, are lightweight and can be susceptible to fire, accidental damage or impact damage to name but a few concerns. There are potential issues with green roofs and walls - if they are not watered enough they can become a fire risk, but if they are watered too much it could cause water damage.
- Transfer of responsibility: Fire-related issues can arise as the MMC manufacturers pass the units to contractors, and fire resistance can be compromised or missed entirely from the framing system.
- Unknown repair costs: As a relatively new method of construction, there is a nervousness around the susceptibility and unknown costs involved when there is damage. Consider a property made of building blocks, and one of those blocks in the middle of the property got damaged - could this block just be removed and replaced, or would half the building have to come down to fix it? In addition, hidden voids that could allow in smoke or water can cause a minor incident becoming a disproportionately large loss.

Issues with pod replacement could cause delays due to removal of a pod and surrounding pods and procurement of replacements to exact specifications. With water damage the entire pod may have to be removed so repairs will not be simple and may be costly.

**Plant Related Concerns:**

- Equipment maintenance: Modern methods of construction often require specialised machinery and plant equipment. Regular maintenance and inspections are essential to ensure safe and efficient operation.
- Training and competence: Handling advanced construction equipment demands skilled operators and workers. Insufficient training or lack of competence in using the machinery can lead to accidents and plant-related liabilities.
- Theft and security: Valuable machinery and equipment on construction sites can attract thieves. Implementing proper security measures is essential to prevent theft and related losses.

To address these hazards and mitigate liability concerns, all parties involved in MMC projects must take proactive measures:

- Conduct thorough risk assessments at each stage of the construction process, including a review of plant maintenance and security.
- Implement stringent quality control measures to ensure the integrity of prefabricated components.
- Ensure that all parties involved - from manufacturers to installers - are adequately trained and experienced and maintain the same level of quality control.
- Maintain open communication among all stakeholders to address potential issues promptly.
- Obtain comprehensive insurance coverage, including liability, contract works, and plant insurance.
- Comply with relevant regulations and obtain necessary approvals for MMC techniques.

Ultimately, MMC is being encouraged with a view to safer buildings, cost efficiency and time saving benefits, energy efficiency and low carbon emissions as the long term goal. Whilst there are still challenges to consider, research continues to alleviate the risks and help to reach this long-term goal.

# JCT Contracts and other Contract Conditions

## What are Contract Conditions?

Contract conditions and responsibilities are fundamental aspects of any construction project and are the basis of any work undertaken. They define the legal obligations, rights, and duties of the parties involved in the contract.

Contract conditions, often referred to as contract clauses, are the specific terms and provisions written into the contract agreement. They serve as the foundation for the contractual relationship between the parties, establishing the rules and guidelines that govern their interactions during the project.

**Key components** of contract conditions include:

Scope of work: Clearly defines the scope and nature of the work to be performed by the contractor. It outlines the project's objectives, deliverables, and performance standards.

Timeframe: Specifies the project's commencement and completion dates, along with any milestones or interim deadlines.

Payment terms: Outlines how and when the contractor will be paid, including the payment schedule and any conditions for payment.

Variations: Addresses the process for making changes to the scope of work, the associated costs, and the approval procedure for variations.

Dispute resolution: Establishes mechanisms for resolving disputes that may arise during the project, such as through mediation or arbitration.

Insurance and indemnity: Outlines the insurance requirements for all parties and addresses indemnification for potential damages or liabilities.

Termination: Specifies the conditions under which either party may terminate the contract.

The contract conditions also detail the responsibilities and duties that each party is expected to fulfil during the project.

**Typical responsibilities** include:

Employer/Client: The majority of the time, the employer is responsible for providing clear project requirements, necessary access to the site, and timely approvals for changes. They must also make timely payments and ensure the contractor has the required permits and approvals to commence work. Sometimes, it is the responsibility of the main contractor to arrange these, where the Employer has no experience of design and build, and is only a financial benefactor.

Contractor: The contractor is responsible for executing the work according to the agreed-upon specifications, meeting quality standards, and adhering to the project schedule. They must also ensure the safety of workers and compliance with all applicable laws and regulations. They must also oversee the subcontractors if they employ any.

Design: In some contracts, the responsibility for design work may fall on either the employer or the contractor, depending on the type of contract used.

Subcontractor: If subcontractors are involved, they have specific responsibilities for their portion of the work, subject to the terms of their subcontract agreements.

Clear definition and understanding of responsibilities are crucial for the successful completion of a construction project. A well-drafted contract with comprehensive contract conditions and clearly defined responsibilities helps minimise disputes, ensure project accountability, and facilitate effective project management. It is essential for all parties to thoroughly review and comprehend their obligations before entering into any construction contract. The writing and agreement of the contract conditions can be a lengthy process with solicitors involved in most steps of the process.

## What are JCT Contracts?

JCT contracts, short for Joint Contracts Tribunal contracts, are a suite of standard forms of building contracts commonly used in the construction industry. The JCT is a collaborative organisation formed by various professional institutions representing the construction industry, including architects, engineers, and contractors. Its primary purpose is to produce and update standard contracts that help regulate relationships and responsibilities among different parties involved in construction projects.

JCT contracts are widely recognised and respected for their fairness, clarity, and balanced allocation of risk between the parties. They are designed to provide a structured framework for managing construction projects, outlining the rights and obligations of the employer, contractor, and other stakeholders throughout the project lifecycle. There are various types of JCT contracts, each tailored to suit different types and sizes of construction projects. Some of the most common JCT contracts include:

- JCT Standard Building Contract (SBC): This is one of the most widely used contracts and is suitable for a wide range of construction projects, including new builds and refurbishments.
- JCT Design and Build Contract (DB): This contract places the design responsibility on the contractor, making it particularly suitable for projects where the employer wants a single point of responsibility for both design and construction.

- JCT Minor Works Contract (MW): This contract is suitable for smaller, less complex projects, providing a more straightforward framework for managing these works.
- JCT Intermediate Building Contract (IC): This contract is designed for projects of intermediate size and complexity.
- JCT Management Building Contract (MC): This contract allows the employer to manage the project directly while using a construction manager to coordinate and oversee the construction works.

JCT contracts cover various aspects of a construction project, including payment terms, project completion dates, performance standards, variations, and dispute resolution procedures. These contracts are regularly updated to reflect changes in industry practices and regulations.

In all JCT contracts, safety and compliance with relevant laws and regulations are paramount. The contractor has the responsibility to ensure the safety of workers and visitors to the construction site, adhering to health and safety regulations. The employer, on the other hand, may have specific responsibilities related to obtaining necessary permits and approvals.

By using JCT contracts, parties involved in construction projects can have greater clarity on their roles, responsibilities, and risks, leading to more efficient project management and reduced potential for disputes. However, it is essential for all parties to fully understand the specific contract they are using and seek professional advice if needed to ensure a successful and legally compliant project.

## Collateral Warranties

Collateral warranties are agreements that provide third parties with direct contractual rights and obligations related to a construction project. These warranties are supplementary to the primary contract and aim to extend the scope of liability to additional parties involved in the project, such as financiers, purchasers, or tenants, who have a vested interest in the construction project but are not a party to the original contract. By obtaining a collateral warranty, these third parties can directly claim against contractors, subcontractors, or consultants if there are defects or failures in the work.

Collateral warranties often mirror the obligations and liabilities of the original contract, ensuring that the third party has similar rights to claim for defects, delays, or other breaches. The warranty will specify its duration, often aligned with the statutory limitation period for construction defects, typically 6-12 years.

Contractors must review their insurance policies to ensure they cover claims under collateral warranties. These would normally be picked up under a Professional Indemnity policy, however cover is likely to need extended to include this as it will be excluded as standard. Protection will not be provided under Public Liability insurance, however for clarity insurers will often apply a Professional Indemnity Exclusion.

# What are HSE Regulations?

The Health and Safety Executive (HSE) is a regulatory body responsible for enforcing health and safety laws in the workplace. The HSE regulations encompass a wide range of rules and guidelines designed to ensure the safety and well-being of workers and the public.

## Construction (Design and Management) Regulations 2015 (CDM)

These are regulations that apply specifically to the construction industry and are designed to improve health and safety management throughout the entire lifecycle of a construction project, from its inception to completion and subsequent maintenance. The CDM Regulations aim to reduce accidents, enhance co-operation and communication among project stakeholders, and ensure that health and safety considerations are integrated into the planning and execution of construction work. Let's have a look at the key components of the CDM Regulations.

### Duty Holders

The regulations introduce specific roles and responsibilities for different parties involved in a construction project. The main duty holders typically include:

- Client: The individual or organisation for whom the construction project is carried out.
- Principal Designer: Appointed to plan, manage, monitor, and coordinate health and safety during the pre-construction phase.
- Principal/Main Contractor: Responsible for planning, managing, monitoring, and coordinating health and safety during the construction phase.

- Main Contractor/sub contractors: Engaged to undertake the actual construction work.

**Pre-Construction Information**

The regulations emphasise the need for the client to provide relevant health and safety information about the project to designers and contractors. This information helps in identifying and managing risks effectively.

**Health and Safety Planning**

The Principal Designer is responsible for creating a health and safety plan during the pre-construction phase where there is expected to be more than one contractor. The Principal Contractor then develops a construction phase plan. These plans outline how health and safety risks will be managed throughout the project.

**Competence**

Duty holders are required to assess and ensure the competence of individuals and organisations involved in the project. This includes designers, contractors, and other relevant parties.

**Risk Management**

The regulations emphasise the importance of identifying, assessing, and managing health and safety risks throughout the project. This includes considering the design, construction, and maintenance phases.

**Communication and Cooperation**

Effective communication and cooperation between duty holders are essential. The regulations encourage collaboration and the sharing of health and safety information to ensure a unified approach to risk management.

**Review and Assessment**

Duty holders are required to review and, if necessary, revise health and safety plans throughout the project. Additionally, a health and safety file is compiled, providing information to facilitate future maintenance, repair, and demolition activities.

Here's how the connection between the HSE and the CDM Regulations works:

## Notification

The CDM Regulations require certain construction projects to be notified to the HSE. This notification is typically the responsibility of the client, the Principal Designer, or the Principal Contractor. The purpose is to inform the HSE about the project and allow for regulatory oversight.

## Enforcement and Inspections

The HSE has the authority to enforce compliance with the CDM Regulations. Inspectors from the HSE may conduct site visits and inspections to ensure that duty holders are fulfilling their obligations under the regulations.

## Guidance and Resources

The HSE provides comprehensive guidance and resources related to the CDM Regulations. This includes publications, toolkits, and informational materials to assist duty holders in understanding and implementing the regulations effectively.

## Prosecution and Penalties

If a construction project is found to be in breach of the CDM Regulations, the HSE has the authority to take enforcement action, including prosecution and the imposition of penalties. Penalties may include fines or, in severe cases, imprisonment.

## Promotion of Best Practices

The HSE actively promotes best practices in health and safety within the construction industry. This includes disseminating information, conducting awareness campaigns, and collaborating with industry stakeholders to improve overall safety standards.

## Review of Notifications

The HSE reviews notifications submitted for certain construction projects to assess the information provided and ensure that duty

holders are fulfilling their responsibilities under the CDM
Regulations.

**Reporting Incidents**

Duty holders are required to report certain incidents, injuries, or
dangerous occurrences to the HSE. This reporting helps the HSE
monitor trends, investigate incidents, and take corrective actions to
prevent future occurrences.


**Key Regulations**

Here are some other key regulations that the HSE enforces. It's
important to note that these regulations are subject to updates and
amendments. Employers and individuals responsible for health and
safety should regularly check for the latest guidance and
regulations provided by the HSE:

*Health and Safety at Work Act 1974 (HSWA)*

This is the primary piece of legislation that outlines the general
duties of employers, employees, and others in ensuring health and
safety at work. It sets the foundation for subsequent regulations
and is a cornerstone of health and safety law.

*Management of Health and Safety at Work Regulations 1999*

These regulations elaborate on the requirements for risk
assessments, policies, and procedures to manage health and safety
effectively in the workplace. They emphasise the need for
competent individuals to carry out risk assessments and implement
control measures.

*Workplace (Health, Safety and Welfare) Regulations 1992*

These regulations focus on the practical aspects of maintaining a
safe and healthy workplace environment. They cover issues such
as ventilation, lighting, cleanliness, facilities, and general welfare
provisions.

## Manual Handling Operations Regulations 1992

These regulations address the risks associated with manual handling activities, providing guidelines on how to assess and reduce the risk of injury when lifting, carrying, or moving loads.

## Personal Protective Equipment at Work Regulations 1992

These regulations outline the requirements for the selection, provision, and use of personal protective equipment (PPE) in the workplace. They ensure that employers assess the need for PPE and provide suitable equipment to protect workers.

## Control of Substances Hazardous to Health Regulations 2002 (COSHH)

COSHH regulations focus on the control of exposure to hazardous substances. They require employers to assess the risks, prevent or control exposure, and provide information, instruction, and training to employees working with hazardous substances.

## Dangerous Substances and Explosive Atmospheres Regulations (DSEAR)

These regulations aim to protect workers from risks related to dangerous substances that could create explosive atmospheres in the workplace. They require employers to assess and control the risks associated with the presence of flammable gases, liquids, dusts, and vapours, and to implement measures to prevent explosions and minimise the consequences of any incidents.

## Provision and Use of Work Equipment Regulations 1998 (PUWER)

PUWER regulations focus on the safe use of work equipment. They require employers to ensure that work equipment is suitable, maintained, and used by trained personnel.

*Reporting of Injuries, Diseases and Dangerous Occurrences*
*Regulations 2013 (RIDDOR)*

RIDDOR regulations mandate the reporting of specified workplace incidents, injuries, diseases, and dangerous occurrences.

Employers, the self-employed, and individuals in control of work premises are required to report incidents to the HSE.

*Electricity at Work Regulations 1989*

These regulations focus on electrical safety in the workplace. They require precautions to be taken against the risk of death or personal injury from electricity in work activities.

## Construction Industry Advisory Committee (CONIAC)

This is a key advisory body established by the HSE, and its primary purpose is to provide expert advice and guidance to the HSE on matters related to health and safety in the construction sector. It aims to improve safety standards, reduce workplace accidents, and ensure compliance with health and safety regulations.

It provides insights and recommendations for the development of health and safety policies specific to the construction industry, and assists in the formulation and revision of health and safety regulations to keep them relevant and effective.

It promotes best practices by developing and disseminating guidelines, case studies, and resources to help construction companies improve their safety practices. CONIAC also supports initiatives aimed at educating workers and employers about health and safety risks and how to mitigate them.

CONIAC ensures stakeholder collaboration and engages with employers, employees, trade unions, and professional bodies, to gather diverse perspectives and foster collaborative efforts. It also organises workshops, forums, and meetings to discuss emerging issues, share knowledge, and develop collective solutions.

Another function of CONIAC is to review and analyse accident and incident data to identify trends, common hazards, and areas needing improvement. It will also produce reports on the state of health and safety in the construction industry, highlighting achievements and ongoing challenges.

CONIAC is composed of representatives from a wide range of organisations within the construction industry, including:

- Employers and Contractors: Major construction firms and industry associations.
- Trade Unions: Representing the interests of construction workers.
- Professional Bodies: Organisations such as the Institution of Occupational Safety and Health (IOSH) and the Royal Institution of Chartered Surveyors (RICS).
- Government Agencies: Representatives from the HSE and other relevant governmental bodies.

The signifiance of this body is that it improves safety standards and ensures regulatory compliance, making sure the H&S regulations are practical, enforceable, and reflective of current industry practices.

**Construction Industry Advisory Network**

CONIAN is a relatively newer entity related to the construction industry. It is an initiative established by the HSE to enhance the focus on health and safety within the construction sector.

CONIAN was established to broaden the engagement with the construction industry, particularly with smaller businesses and the self-employed, to promote health and safety awareness and compliance. Its goal is to complement the work of the CONIAC by extending outreach and support, and it ensures regional representation and input, addressing local challenges and solutions in construction health and safety.

CONIAN utilises various communication channels to reach a wider audience, including online platforms, workshops, and forums. The initiative provides practical support and resources to help smaller businesses and self-employed workers understand and comply with health and safety regulations. It develops and distributes toolkits, templates, and other practical resources to facilitate health and safety management on construction sites. CONIAN collects feedback from the industry, particularly from those who might not typically have a voice in larger advisory bodies. It uses this feedback to inform the HSE and influence health and safety policy and regulatory developments. It also offers cost-effective solutions and guidance tailored to the capabilities and needs of smaller entities.

## HSE inspections and notices

I briefly mentioned above regarding enforcement actions. As a regulator, the HSE has various approaches to ensuring safe living and working environments. One such approach is an HSE inspection. In the case of contractors, this will tend to be on contract sites rather than their own premises. These tend to be unplanned in an effort to review the current state of Health & Safety, rather than a contractor having time to prepare something in advance - the idea is not to catch them out, but to ensure they have good working practices in place already, and to give targeted advice if needed. The aim is to prevent any incidents, however they will enforce the law where it is not being followed. This often involves serving notices on companies or individuals, and following up to ensure the necessary actions have been taken within the timescales given.

**Prohibition Notice** - Issued to prohibit certain activities or processes that pose a significant risk to health and safety. It is served when the HSE believes that there is a risk of serious injury or harm that needs immediate attention and must be rectified urgently. Failure to comply with a Prohibition Notice is a criminal offense and can lead to fines or imprisonment.

**Improvement Notice** - Issued to the recipient to remedy certain health and safety issues within a specified timeframe. It is served when the HSE identifies non-compliance with health and safety laws that do not pose an immediate and serious risk but still need to be addressed. It specifies the actions that need to be taken to address the identified health and safety issues and provides a reasonable timeframe within which the improvements must be made. Failure to comply with an Improvement Notice is also a criminal offense and can lead to fines.

Duty holders have the right to appeal against these notices if they believe them to be unjust or unreasonable.

The HSE publishes information regarding the notices served, and it is available to view on their website. These notices are crucial tools for the HSE to enforce health and safety regulations, ensure compliance, and protect the well-being of workers in various workplaces. They play a key role in promoting a culture of safety and accountability within organisations.

The HSE website is a very useful source of information for the insurance industry - whether it is checking on HSE notices, reading up on current legislation, or assisting clients in their Health and Safety procedures and documentation - there is a wealth of information and templates to assist businesses, brokers and insurance companies.

# General Risk Management for Liability

Risk management is a crucial aspect of any construction project. It involves a systematic approach to identifying, assessing, and mitigating potential risks that could lead to accidents, injuries, or other harmful incidents. Let's explore how a robust risk management process, starting with health and safety policies, risk assessments, and method statements, contributes to liability reduction.

## Competent Person

A Competent Person can be an individual within a company that is qualified and experienced to produce, oversee and monitor the Health and Safety procedures within a company. If the company does not have a qualified person for this role, they may use external Health & Safety consultants instead.

## Health and Safety Policy

A health and safety policy is the cornerstone of risk management in construction. It is a formal statement by the employer or main contractor that outlines their commitment to ensuring a safe working environment for all involved in the project. The policy sets the overall objectives for health and safety and defines the responsibilities of key personnel.

The policy should communicate the company's dedication to adhering to health and safety regulations, providing adequate resources, and fostering a culture of safety throughout the organisation. A companies Health and Safety policy should be reviewed on an annual basis, and shared with all employees. A *written* Health and Safety Policy is required where a company has five or more employees. Whilst it is not a legal requirement for a company with less employees to have a written policy, it is still a recommendation. Smaller companies must have a minimum of a verbal H&S policy which is communicated to all staff members so it is clear what their Health & Safety approach is and who is responsible.

## Risk Assessments

Risk assessments are a systematic evaluation of potential hazards and risks associated with specific activities or tasks on the contract site. These assessments involve identifying hazards, evaluating their severity and likelihood, and implementing appropriate controls to reduce or eliminate the risks. Risk assessments cover a wide range of hazards, such as working at height, handling hazardous materials, using heavy machinery, and potential exposure to electrical hazards. Regular and thorough risk assessments help prevent accidents and demonstrate a proactive approach to liability management.

## Method Statements

Often carried out alongside risk assessments, method statements provide detailed procedures for specific tasks or activities on the contract site. They outline how the work will be carried out safely, considering the identified hazards and the control measures to be implemented.

Method statements address aspects such as the sequence of work, safety precautions, use of personal protective equipment (PPE), and emergency procedures. These documents ensure that all workers and contractors understand the safe working practices and responsibilities associated with their tasks, reducing the risk of accidents and potential liability claims.

Risk assessments and method statements are often referred to as **RAMS.**

## Training and Competency

Proper training and competency assessments are vital for ensuring that workers have the necessary skills and knowledge to perform their tasks safely. Regular training updates keep workers informed about the latest safety practices and regulations. This includes specific training related to their trade and activities, which I will cover in more detail later, as well as general health and safety training.

## Toolbox Talks

Toolbox talks are short, informal safety meetings that are typically held on construction sites to discuss specific health and safety topics and address potential hazards. These talks are an essential part of a company's health and safety program and are often conducted before the start of a shift or work activity. The purpose of toolbox talks include the following:

- Raising awareness about specific health and safety issues relevant to the work being undertaken, such as hazards, risks, and safe work practices.
- Promoting communication, by encouraging open communication among workers, supervisors, and management regarding safety concerns, observations, and suggestions for improvement.
- Serving as a form of ongoing training by reinforcing safety procedures, protocols, and best practices related to the tasks at hand.
- To help prevent accidents, injuries, and near misses in the workplace, by addressing potential hazards and emphasizing safe work practices.

Key components:

- Topic selection: Could include fall protection, electrical safety, personal protective equipment (PPE), or hazard communication.
- Presentation & discussion: Toolbox talks are typically brief, lasting no more than ten to fifteen minutes, to keep workers engaged and attentive. They may include visual aids, such as posters, diagrams, or videos, to reinforce key points. They encourage interactive discussion among participants, allowing them to share their experiences, ask questions, and provide input on safety-related issues.
- Action items: Toolbox talks often conclude with action items or takeaways for workers to implement, such as inspecting equipment, using proper PPE, or reporting hazards to supervisors.

**Benefits of Toolbox Talks**

Toolbox talks help workers stay informed about potential hazards and safe work practices, leading to increased awareness and vigilance on the job. They facilitate communication and collaboration among workers, supervisors, and management, fostering a culture of safety and accountability. Toolbox talks help organisations meet regulatory requirements and demonstrate their commitment to health and safety compliance in the workplace.

As well as carrying out toolbox talks, thorough documentation should be kept in case of any incidents that may arise. Records could include topics discussed, attendance, and any action items identified, to track progress and ensure accountability.

## Provision and Enforcement of Using Personal Protective Equipment (PPE)

Personal Protective Equipment (PPE) is essential for safeguarding workers from specific workplace hazards. A comprehensive risk management strategy includes identifying the appropriate PPE required for each task or activity and ensuring its provision to all workers. This includes items such as hard hats, safety goggles, gloves, and high-visibility vests, as well as specialised equipment specific to the trade or activity, such as harnesses for working at height.

Proper enforcement of PPE usage is critical to mitigating liability risks. Site supervisors and managers should actively monitor and enforce the wearing of PPE to prevent accidents and injuries. Many companies require workers to sign for PPE to ensure they understand how to use the equipment and to acknowledge that they will use it. Non-compliance with PPE requirements would be addressed promptly through training and disciplinary measures.

## Accident Investigation Procedures and RIDDOR

Accidents, unfortunately, can still occur despite risk management efforts. In such cases, a robust accident investigation procedure is vital for understanding the cause of the incident and implementing corrective actions to prevent similar occurrences in the future.

Promptly reporting accidents and near-miss incidents is crucial. An investigation team should be assembled to gather evidence, interview witnesses, and analyse the root causes of the accident. RIDDOR reporting must be carried out where required.

The findings of accident investigations should be documented, and actions taken to prevent recurrence should be communicated to all relevant parties.

**What is RIDDOR?**

RIDDOR, or the Reporting of Injuries, Diseases, and Dangerous Occurrences Regulations, is a legal framework that mandates employers, self-employed individuals, and those overseeing work sites to report specified work-related incidents to the HSE. These reports provide a critical view of accidents, illnesses, and potential hazards within different industries and oversees the protection of workers and the public.

**What needs to be reported?**

- Work-related fatalities: Any death arising out of or in connection with work.
- Specified injuries to workers: These include fractures (except fingers, thumbs, and toes), amputations, any injury likely to lead to permanent loss of sight or reduction of sight, crush injuries to the head or torso causing damage to the brain or internal organs, serious burns, scalping requiring hospital treatment, loss of consciousness caused by head injury or asphyxia, and any other injury arising from working in an enclosed space leading to hypothermia or heat-induced illness, or requiring resuscitation or admittance to hospital for more than 24 hours.
- Over-seven-day injuries: Injuries that lead to a worker being incapacitated for more than seven consecutive days.
- Injuries to non-workers: Injuries to members of the public or people not at work (but which involve a work activity) that result in them being taken directly to hospital for treatment. This does not include incidents where the person is taken to hospital as a precaution or where only examinations or diagnostic tests are undertaken
- Occupational diseases: These include carpal tunnel syndrome, severe cramp of the hand or forearm,

occupational dermatitis, hand-arm vibration syndrome, occupational asthma, tendonitis or tenosynovitis of the hand or forearm, any occupational cancer, and any disease attributed to an occupational exposure to a biological agent.

- Dangerous occurrences: These are specified near-miss events, such as the collapse, overturning or failure of load-bearing parts of lifts and lifting equipment, explosions or fires causing work to be stopped for more than 24 hours, accidental release of a biological agent likely to cause severe human illness, and other serious incidents that could have resulted in harm.

- Gas incidents: The following requires to be reported if it has resulted in someone dying, losing consciousness, or being taken to hospital for treatment: Gas leaks, carbon monoxide poisoning, gas-related injuries or dangerous gas fittings. Gas Safe registered engineers must report any dangerous gas fittings or appliances they encounter that pose a serious risk to health and safety, including at domestic premises.

**Duty and Accountability: The Reporting Process**

When a reportable incident occurs, duty holders have a legal obligation to promptly notify the HSE through the appropriate channels. Fatal accidents and major incidents should be reported immediately by telephone. All other reportable injuries and incidents should be reported within 10 days of the incident, and occupational diseasess should be reported as soon as a doctor confirms the diagnosis.

The primary duty falls on employers to report relevant incidents, and self-employed individuals must report incidents affecting themselves. Owners or occupiers of premises are responsible for reporting incidents involving non-workers. There should be a designated person within an organisation that is responsible for reporting incidents, this can include health and safety officers, managers, or other designated individuals.

Reports can be made to the HSE via their online reporting system, by phone for fatalities and major incidents, or by completing the appropriate RIDDOR form and sending it to the HSE.

## Health Checks

Regular health checks - systematic and routine examinations or assessments aimed at monitoring and promoting the health and well-being of employees - are part of a proactive approach to identify and manage potential health risks in the workplace, contributing to a safer and healthier working environment. This can include exposure to hazardous substances, ergonomic concerns, noise levels, and other factors that may impact employee health.

Key aspects of regular health checks under health and safety include:

### Prevention and Early Detection

Regular health checks are a preventive measure designed to identify health issues at an early stage. Early detection allows for timely intervention and management, reducing the risk of more serious health problems developing over time.

For example, where vibration is a particular concern for employees, there are watches that can be worn by the employee that will monitor the amount of vibration they experience whilst using tools. This will help avoid exceeding recommended daily allowances.

### Occupational Health Assessments

Occupational health assessments are a common component of regular health checks. These assessments evaluate how the work environment may be affecting employees' physical and mental health. They may include assessments of posture, vision, hearing, and exposure to specific workplace hazards.

### Legal and Regulatory Compliance

There are legal and regulatory requirements for employers to conduct regular health checks, especially in industries where specific health risks are prevalent. Compliance with these requirements is essential to ensure a safe and healthy workplace.

### Record-Keeping

Employers typically maintain records of health checks for each employee. These records help track changes in health status over time, monitor the effectiveness of preventive measures, and demonstrate compliance with health and safety regulations.

### Integrating Results into Risk Management

The results of health checks are integral to the risk management process. Employers can use the information obtained to implement targeted interventions, such as adjusting work processes, providing PPE, or offering health and safety training.

## The Importance of Keeping Documentation

Documentation is an integral part of risk management and liability reduction. Maintaining comprehensive and up-to-date records of all risk assessments, method statements, safety training sessions, incident reports, and accident investigations is essential for several reasons:

*Compliance and Legal Requirements:* Proper documentation demonstrates compliance with health and safety regulations, industry standards, and contractual obligations. Contractors must comply with relevant health and safety regulations in the UK, and specific regulations related to their trade or activity. In the event of a liability claim or dispute, well-documented records serve as evidence of responsible and diligent risk management.

*Due Diligence:* Maintaining meticulous records is a demonstration of due diligence on the part of the employer or main contractor. It shows that all reasonable steps were taken to prevent accidents and ensure a safe working environment.

*Learning and Improvement:* Documentation helps facilitate learning from past experiences. By analysing records, trends, and patterns, construction companies can identify areas for improvement and implement better safety practices.

*Contractual and Insurance Purposes:* Many construction contracts require specific documentation as part of their compliance requirements. Additionally, insurance companies may request documentation to assess liability claims, which can be crucial for claims defence.

## Statutory Inspections
All plant used and supplied must have statutory inspections as well as regular pre-use checks, and only used as per the manufacturers instructions.

## Continuous Monitoring and Review
Effective risk management is an ongoing process. Regular site inspections, incident investigations, and reviews of safety procedures help identify any new hazards or areas for improvement. Monitoring and reviewing risk management efforts ensure that safety measures remain relevant and effective

throughout the project's duration. Complacency is likely to result in accidents. By implementing and continually reviewing a comprehensive risk management approach, liability risks are reduced and a culture of safety is promoted throughout the organisation. A safe and well-managed contract site not only protects the well-being of workers and the public but also safeguards the reputation and financial interests of all stakeholders involved.

# Risk Management from a Contract Works Perspective

Risk management at contract sites involves a comprehensive approach to identify and mitigate potential hazards and risks throughout the construction project. It encompasses various aspects, including fire safety, site and plant security, and adherence to specific standards, such as JCOP (Joint Code of Practice) guidelines. Let's explore each of these elements in more detail.

## Fire Safety

Fire safety is a critical concern on construction sites due to the presence of flammable materials, equipment, and temporary structures. A robust fire risk assessment should be conducted to identify potential ignition sources, fuel sources, and methods to prevent or control fires.

Fire prevention measures may include proper storage of flammable materials, use of fire-resistant construction materials, and the implementation of a site-wide fire safety plan.

Firefighting equipment, such as fire extinguishers, hose reels, and fire alarms, should be strategically placed and regularly maintained.

Emergency evacuation procedures and assembly points should be clearly communicated to all workers.

## Site Security

Construction sites are vulnerable to theft, vandalism, and unauthorised access. Proper security measures are essential to safeguard the site, equipment, and materials. Here's an overview of some of the site security options available:

### Perimeter Fencing and Barriers

Perimeter fencing with controlled access points helps restrict entry to authorised personnel only. Portable fencing (such as Heras) can be easily installed and removed, whilst hoarding (solid timber panels) can provide both security and privacy. Anti-climb fencing is designed to be difficult to scale. Vehicle barriers such as gates or bollards are used to control vehicle access. Physical security deters unauthorised entry and clearly defines site boundaries.

### CCTV Surveillance

CCTV cameras are used to monitor and record activity on the construction site. They can be used for live monitoring, or record footage for future review. Motion detection triggers recording or alerts the owner. These act as a deterrent to theft and vandalism, can provide evidence in case of such an incident, and enhance overall site security.

### Security Lighting

Motion activated lighting can be installed to illuminate the construction site, particularly during non-working hours. This can deters potential intruders, enhance visibility for CCTV cameras, and reduce the risk of accidents.

### Security Guards

Employing trained personnel to patrol and monitor the construction site can deter potential trespassers and intruders. Regular patrols can check for security breaches, managing entry and exit points, and will be able to immediately respond to security incidents. Where security guards are utilised, it is often round-the-clock presence to ensure site security.

### Access Control Systems

Electronic systems can be used to control and monitor access to the construction site, using keycards or fobs. Larger construction sites or those in higher risk areas may use more advanced technology such as biometric systems, using fingerprint or facial recognition to allow access. Turnstiles can be used as controlled entry points that allow only one person at a time. There should also be visitor management systems to track and manage visitors to the site. This will not only prevent unauthorised access, but it will also track who is on site at any time.

## Alarm Systems

Installed alarm systems can detect and alert to security breaches (intruder alarms), detect smoke and fire (fire alarms), or allow workers to signal emergencies (panic alarms). These alarms can be remotely monitored by a security company, and provide immediate alerts to security breaches.

## Mobile Security Units

Mobile security units, such as security trailers or towers, can be equipped with several types of surveillance equipment - surveillance cameras, security lighting, alarm systems - which can all be remotely monitored and controlled. These provide flexibility as they can be moved as needed, and they provide a comprehensive security solution.

## Plant Security

Plant security is essential to protect valuable construction equipment from theft and misuse. Several types of security measures can be implemented, ranging from basic physical locks (keys, padlocks, chains, etc) to advanced technological innovations. Here's an overview of the various plant security options available:

## GPS Trackers

GPS trackers are devices that use satellite technology to monitor and report the location of plant equipment in real time. It alerts the necessary person if the equipment moves outside a predefined area (geofencing). It can track and record the equipment's movement history, and can be remotely monitored via web or mobile apps. They can help recover stolen equipment quickly.

### Immobilizers

Immobilizers are electronic devices that prevent plant equipment from being started without proper authorisation. They can be activated or deactivated remotely, and are engaged automatically when equipment is not in use.They are often linked with alarm systems to enhance security. This helps prevent unauthorised use, reduces the risk of theft, and enhances control over equipment usage.

### Anti-Theft Alarms

These are alarms that trigger an alert if unauthorised access, tampering or movement is detected, through the use of motion sensors. They can emit a loud noise or send a silent alert to the owner. These alarms can be integrated with other security measures like trackers and immobilizers. They deter potential thieves, alert owners or security personnel of suspicious activity, and can be monitored remotely.

### Security Marking and Registration

High-value plant and equipment should be marked with identification numbers and registered on national databases to aid recovery in case of theft. Plant may be visibly marked by engraving or labelling them with unique ID numbers, or invisibly marked using substances like SmartWater or microdots that are visible under UV light. Marking makes equipment less attractive to thieves, aids in the identification and recovery of stolen equipment, and deters resale of stolen equipment.

### Biometric Access Control

Uses biometric data (like fingerprints or facial recognition) to control access to equipment, which ensures only authorised personnel can operate the equipment. Audit trails record access logs for accountability. They can be integrated with GPS trackers and immobilizers. BAC can prevent unauthorised use, enhance accountability and security, and provide detailed access logs. Implementing a combination of these security measures can significantly enhance the protection of plant equipment. The choice of security measures will depend on the specific needs, budget, and operational requirements of the construction site. Some insurers work in conjunction with security providers to assist with security products, and in turn the use of these by construction companies can effectively safeguard their valuable assets from theft and misuse and reduce their insurance premiums.

## Employees Tools

With regards to employees tools, contractors should provide secure storage areas on sites, and promote employee awareness of theft prevention strategies. Regular inspections of tools and equipment, proper maintenance procedures, and employee training on the safe use and storage of personal belongings can also help mitigate risks and minimise losses.

## Joint Code of Practice - Fire Prevention on Construction Sites

The Joint Code of Practice (JCoP) on Fire Prevention on Construction Sites is a comprehensive guideline developed to minimise fire risks during construction and renovation projects. JCOP first published these guidelines in 1992, with the most recent version (10.1) being published in January 2023. Whilst it still covers some long standing activities such as hot work, it also addresses some of the more modern material usage and construction practises, such as electric vehicle charging. Generally it applies to contracts with a value of more than £2.5m, however it may also apply to lower value contracts which are considered high risk, or which form part of a larger project (£20m or above). For smaller contracts, where it is not a requirement for the contract or insurance purposes, it is considered 'best practice'.

JCOP outlines the requirements for preventing, detecting, and fighting fires on construction sites. The code emphasises measures such as the use of fire-resistant materials, early detection systems, and the presence of sufficient firefighting equipment. JCOP also covers fire safety training for personnel and the importance of maintaining clear access routes for emergency services. Let's have a look at the key requirements:

### Fire Safety Management

A fire safety plan should be developed specific to the site, detailing fire prevention measures, emergency procedures, and roles and responsibilities. A thorough fire risk assessment should be completed and updated regularly to identify and mitigate potential fire hazards. A Fire Safety Coordinator must be appointed to oversee fire safety management and ensure compliance.

### Site Security and Access

The site must be secured against unauthorised access, and clear access must be maintained for the Fire Brigade at all times.

### Fire Detection and Alarm Systems

Fire detection systems must be installed and maintained that are appropriate for the size and complexity of the site. Alarm systems must be in place and regularly tested to provide early warning in case of fire.

### Means of Escape

Clear escape routes must be designated and maintained, that are free from obstructions and clearly marked. Assembly points must be identified and communicated for site personnel in case of evacuation.

### Fire Fighting Equipment

Provision of an adequate number and type of fire extinguishers, strategically placed around the site. Site personnel must be trained in the use of fire fighting equipment and understand the location and operation of fire extinguishers.

### *Control of Combustible Materials*

Combustible materials must be stored in designated areas away from ignition sources, and limited quantities are allowed to bestored on-site. Procedures must be implemented for the regular removal and safe disposal of waste materials.

### *Hot Work Permits*

A hot work permit system must be inmplemented to control activities such as welding, cutting, and grinding, and such work must be supervised and monitored, and that appropriate fire safety measures are in place.

### *Temporary Buildings and Accommodation*

Temporary buildings and accommodation must be positioned away from high-risk areas and constructed from fire-resistant materials. Temporary structures should be equipped with appropriate fire detection, alarm systems, and fire fighting equipment.

### *Emergency Procedures*

An evacuation plan should be developed to include roles and responsibilities, and communicated to site personnel. Regular fire drills should be conducted to ensure all personnel are familiar with emergency procedures and can evacuate quickly and safely.

### *Liaison with Fire Authorities*

Regular communication and coordination with local fire authorities should be maintained to ensure they are aware of site-specific risks and have access to necessary information.

There is an interesting Excerpt from the latest version that is worth noting:
"If compliance with this Code forms part of the insurance contract, non-compliance with this Code could possibly result in insurance

ceasing to be available or being withdrawn, resulting in a possible breach of a construction contract which requires the provision of such insurance."

# Accreditations

Construction accreditations ensure that individuals, companies, and projects within the construction industry adhere to specific standards and regulations. Here's an explanation of some widely recognised construction accreditations:

## CSCS (Construction Skills Certification Scheme) card Certification

CSCS cards verify the skills and qualifications of construction workers.

Individuals must pass the CITB Health, Safety and Environment (HS&E) test relevant to their role prior to the CSCS certification. This test evaluates a candidate's understanding of health, safety, and environmental issues in the construction sector.

Widely recognised in the industry, the card demonstrates competence and commitment to safety. Whilst it is not a legal requirement, it tends to be a minimum requirement specified by principal contractors for workers to be permitted on site.

## CITB Health and Safety Awareness

A training course providing essential health and safety knowledge for individuals entering the construction industry, it is often a prerequisite for obtaining a CSCS card. This equips individuals with foundational safety knowledge before entering construction sites.

## CHAS (Contractors Health and Safety Assessment Scheme)

CHAS assesses the health and safety competence of contractors and service providers. It demonstrates compliance with health and safety legislation and best practices and indicates a commitment to high standards of health and safety management.

## Constructionline

This is a procurement and supply chain management service that simplifies the process of contractor and supplier selection. The entry process for this is an evaluation of a company's financial health, technical capabilities, and adherence to industry standards. This accreditation streamlines the prequalification process, saving time and resources for both buyers and suppliers.

## Safe Contractor

Safe Contractor is a health and safety accreditation scheme recognising high standards in health and safety management, and companies must be assessed on the effectiveness of their health and safety practices. This accreditation provides evidence of a commitment to maintaining a safe working environment.

## SMSTS (Site Management Safety Training Scheme)

A training course for construction site managers and supervisors, SMSTS focuses on health and safety responsibilities. This is typically taken by those in managerial roles, which equips managers with the knowledge and skills to ensure safe practices on construction sites.

## ISO (International Organisation for Standardisation)

ISO is a series of standards that outline criteria for quality, safety, and efficiency in various industries, including construction. To be ISO accredited, a company must comply with specific ISO standards, such as ISO 9001 for quality management. This indicates adherence to internationally recognised standards, enhancing credibility and competitiveness.

### *Why is ISO9001 good for the construction industry?*

ISO 9001 is a globally recognised standard for quality management systems, and its adoption in the construction industry offers several benefits that contribute to improved efficiency, enhanced customer satisfaction, and overall excellence in project delivery. Here are key reasons why ISO 9001 is advantageous for the construction industry:

*Quality Management*

- ISO 9001 helps construction companies establish consistent and standardised processes, ensuring that quality is maintained throughout all stages of a project.
- The standard emphasises the importance of Quality Control to identify and address potential issues, leading to higher quality outcomes.

*Customer Satisfaction*

- ISO 9001 focuses on understanding and meeting customer requirements. In the construction industry, this translates to delivering projects that align with client expectations in terms of quality, budget, and timelines.
- Improved quality management reduces the likelihood of defects and the need for rework, contributing to higher customer satisfaction.

*Efficiency and Cost Savings*

- ISO 9001 encourages the optimisation of processes, leading to increased efficiency and reduced waste in construction projects.
- By minimising errors and rework, construction companies can control costs more effectively, resulting in improved financial performance.

*Risk Management*

- Identification and Mitigation of Risks: The standard prompts organisations to identify and mitigate risks in their processes. In construction, this includes anticipating potential issues related to safety, regulatory compliance, and project delays.
- Proactive Problem Solving: ISO 9001 promotes a proactive approach to addressing risks, allowing construction companies to mitigate issues before they escalate.

*Regulatory Compliance*

- ISO 9001 assists construction companies in ensuring that their processes comply with relevant legal and regulatory requirements. This is especially crucial in an industry with stringent safety and building code regulations.

*Improved Communication*

- The standard encourages the establishment of clear communication channels within organisations. In construction, effective communication between project teams, contractors, and stakeholders is vital for successful project execution.

*Continuous Improvement*

- ISO 9001 promotes the Plan-Do-Check-Act (PDCA) cycle, fostering a culture of continuous improvement. Construction companies can systematically identify areas for enhancement and implement changes to enhance overall performance.

*Competitive Advantage*

- ISO 9001 certification signals a commitment to quality and customer satisfaction. This can enhance the reputation of construction firms, making them more competitive in the market.

- Many clients, especially in large construction projects, prefer working with ISO 9001-certified contractors, providing a competitive advantage when bidding for contracts.

Here are some other key ISO accreditations that are valuable for the construction sector:

*ISO 14001: Environmental Management System (EMS)*

ISO 14001 helps construction companies establish and maintain an effective environmental management system. This includes assessing and mitigating environmental impacts associated with construction activities, waste management, and resource efficiency. Construction projects can have significant environmental implications, and ISO 14001 certification demonstrates a commitment to sustainable practices.

*ISO 45001 (previously OHSAS 18001): Occupational Health and Safety Management System (OHSMS)*

ISO 45001 provides a framework for managing occupational health and safety risks. Construction sites inherently involve various risks, and this standard helps ensure a safe working environment, reducing accidents and injuries.
Construction projects often involve complex and hazardous work conditions, making occupational health and safety a critical focus area.

*Safe T cert*

Safe T cert is a health and safety management system and certification scheme designed for the construction industry in the UK and the Republic of Ireland. It provides a framework for companies to assess and demonstrate their commitment to ensuring a safe and healthy working environment.

The purpose of Safe T cert is to help construction companies implement effective health and safety management practices. It provides a recognised certification that signifies a company's adherence to high safety standards, promoting a culture of safety within the organisation.

Safe T cert is significant as it enhances the credibility of construction companies by demonstrating their commitment to creating safe workplaces. It may also be a requirement for participating in certain projects, especially those that prioritise safety standards.

### Construction Employers Federation

The CEF is a trade association representing the interests of construction companies in Northern Ireland. It serves as a collective voice for employers in the construction industry, advocating for their needs and concerns.

CEF works to promote and support the interests of its member companies, addressing issues such as legislation, training, and industry best practices. It provides a platform for collaboration and information exchange among construction employers.

Membership in CEF allows construction employers to stay informed about industry developments, participate in advocacy efforts, and access resources and support for their businesses.

You may also come across the following accreditations:

*Chartered Institute of Building (CIOB) Qualification* - cover various aspects of construction management.

*SSIP (Safety Schemes in Procurement)* - assesses health and safety competence of contractors.

*Achilles Building Confidence* - focuses on areas such as health and safety, environmental management, and corporate social responsibility.

*SMAS (Safety Management Advisory Services)* - health and safety assessment scheme.

*CPCS (Construction Plant Competence Scheme)* - certification scheme for plant operators within the construction industry.

*NPORS (National Plant Operators Registration Scheme)* - NPORS is another certification scheme for plant operators.

*Alcumus Safe Contractor* -  A health and safety accreditation scheme, assessing and certifying contractors' health and safety practices, ensuring compliance with industry standards.

*NVQ (National Vocational Qualifications)* - NVQs are work-based qualifications that assess an individual's competence in a specific job role. They are designed to recognise and validate practical skills in various industries, including construction.

*City & Guilds Certifications* - Provider of industry-recognised vocational qualifications covering a wide range of industries including construction, designed to validate the skills and knowledge of individuals.

# Health and Safety Assistance

There are a wide range of Health & Safety courses available, and third party Health & Safety consultants who can assist with the necessary regulatory and industry requirements. Let's have a look at some of the options that are available for H&S assistance.

**IOSH (Institution of Occupational Safety and Health)**

IOSH is a professional organisation that focuses on promoting health and safety in the workplace. It offers various training courses, resources, and membership options for individuals working in diverse industries, including construction. The aim is to enhance knowledge and skills related to occupational safety and health.

Benefits for the construction industry:

- IOSH certifications, such as the Managing Safely and Working Safely courses are recognised professional development that provide construction professionals with essential knowledge and skills to manage safety effectively on construction sites.
- IOSH training ensures that individuals are aware of and understand relevant health and safety laws and regulations, helping companies maintain legal compliance.
- The training emphasises risk assessment and management, crucial in the dynamic and hazard-prone environment of contract sites.
- IOSH fosters a safety-oriented mindset, encouraging individuals in the construction industry to prioritise safety in all aspects of their work.
- IOSH courses targeted at managerial levels equip construction leaders with the tools to lead safety initiatives and create a safer working environment.

## NEBOSH (National Examination Board in Occupational Safety and Health)

NEBOSH is an independent examination board that offers a range of globally recognised qualifications in occupational health and safety. NEBOSH certifications cover various sectors, including construction, providing comprehensive training on health and safety management.

Benefits for the construction industry:

- NEBOSH qualifications are recognised and well-regarded globally, making them valuable for construction professionals working on projects across different countries.
- NEBOSH offers construction-specific certifications like the NEBOSH Construction Certificate, which focuses on the unique risks and challenges in the industry.
- NEBOSH courses equip individuals with skills in identifying and controlling workplace hazards, which is crucial for this risk-diverse sector.
- NEBOSH Diplomas, such as the NEBOSH Diploma in Occupational Health and Safety, are designed for professionals in leadership roles, providing them with in-depth knowledge to lead safety initiatives.
- NEBOSH courses cover relevant legislation and regulations, helping construction professionals stay informed and compliant with safety standards.
- By promoting a strong safety culture and providing practical tools for risk management, NEBOSH certifications contribute to reducing incidents and accidents at contract sites.

**Combined Impact**

Having both IOSH and NEBOSH qualifications can be highly beneficial for individuals in the construction industry. These certifications complement each other by providing a holistic understanding of health and safety, from day-to-day management (IOSH) to in-depth knowledge and leadership (NEBOSH). They contribute to creating a safer, healthier, and more productive construction environment while enhancing individual and organisational credibility in the industry.

## UKATA (United Kingdom Asbestos Training Association) Asbestos Awareness

UKATA is a leading authority in the UK for asbestos training. The UKATA Asbestos Awareness training is designed to provide essential knowledge about asbestos, its risks, and how to work safely in environments where asbestos may be present. Asbestos is a hazardous material that was commonly used in construction before its ban due to health risks. Asbestos Awareness training is crucial for individuals working in the construction and related industries, where the risk of encountering asbestos-containing materials is significant. More information on asbestos is covered later in the book.

### Key Components of UKATA Asbestos Awareness Training

Identification of asbestos: Understanding asbestos types and recognition of Asbestos-Containing Materials (ACMs).

Health risks: The health risks associated with asbestos exposure and the critical role of preventing exposure to asbestos fibres to protect their health.

Regulatory compliance: An overview of relevant UK asbestos regulations, including the Control of Asbestos Regulations 2012. It explains about individuals legal responsibilities when working in or around areas with potential asbestos-containing materials.

Safe working practices: Participants are instructed on how to avoid disturbing ACM during construction or maintenance activities, and the appropriate use of PPE to minimise the risk of asbestos exposure.

Emergency procedures: Guidance on what to do in case of accidental disturbance of asbestos, emphasising immediate reporting and evacuation procedures.

Risk communication: Advice on clear communication regarding the presence of asbestos, ensuring all relevant parties are informed, and understanding the significance of asbestos warning signs and labels.

Benefits of UKATA Asbestos Awareness Training:

- Enhances awareness and understanding of asbestos risks, reducing the likelihood of accidental exposure.
- Ensures compliance with asbestos-related regulations, protecting both individuals and organisations from legal consequences.
- Promotes a culture of health and safety, emphasising the wellbeing of workers and the public.
- Provides individuals with the necessary knowledge and skills to work safely in environments where asbestos may be present.
- Equips workers with the tools to identify and report asbestos-containing materials, contributing to overall risk mitigation.

UKATA Asbestos Awareness training is a fundamental requirement for anyone likely to encounter asbestos during their work in construction, maintenance, or related activities. It plays a crucial role in safeguarding the health and well-being of individuals in the construction industry while ensuring regulatory compliance.

## External H&S Consultants

External Health and Safety consultants are professionals or consulting firms hired by organisations to provide independent expertise, advice, and support in managing health and safety matters in the workplace. These consultants play a crucial role in helping businesses ensure compliance with relevant regulations, create safer working environments, and mitigate risks associated with health and safety issues.

External consultants typically have specialised knowledge and expertise in health and safety regulations, and varied backgrounds, allowing them to address a wide range of health and safety concerns.

Their responsibilities cover:

- Regulatory compliance, including any changes
- Risk assessment and management
- Risk mitigation strategies
- Training and education of management and employees in H&S topics
- Audits and inspections
- Assistance in emergency preparedness
- H&S policy development and documentation
- Assist with incident investigation and reporting in compliance with regulatory requirements
- Continuous improvement
- Legal support

Businesses often engage consultants on a project-by-project basis or as ongoing advisors to enhance their overall health and safety practices, and may nominate them as their Competent Person.

# Hot Work

In the dynamic landscape of occupational environments, certain activities pose heightened risks that demand specialised attention to ensure the health and safety of workers. Specific hazardous activities, including work involving heat, height or depth, operations at hazardous locations, and tasks with hazardous substances, necessitate meticulous risk management strategies. Understanding the unique challenges associated with each of these activities is paramount to creating a workplace environment that prioritises the wellbeing of individuals and minimises the potential for accidents, injuries or damage. Let's start with looking at hot work in detail.

**Unveiling Heat Work: HSE's Definition**

Hot work is any activity that generates flames, sparks or heat. A common misconception is that heat work is only in relation to working with open flames, however the definition is wider than this. According to the HSE it includes welding, cutting, grinding, brazing, soldering, torching and sawing, and in fact any process that generates flames, sparks or heat.

The main hazards of working with heat are worker injuries, third party injuries, and significant property damage.

Let us have a look at some of the heat methods in more detail:

**Welding**

Welding processes are extensively used in the construction industry for joining metal components, creating structural elements, and fabricating various building elements. Each welding method has its advantages and disadvantages, and the choice depends on factors such as the project requirements, material type, thickness, and desired weld characteristics. Here's an overview of some of the common welding processes used in construction, their main uses, and their pros and cons:

*Shielded metal arc welding (Stick welding)*

An arc is created between a flux-coated electrode and the workpiece, forming a protective shield of gas and slag.

Advantages: Portable and suitable for outdoor applications, versatile and applicable to various materials.

Disadvantages: Slower deposition rates (rate of melting) compared to some other processes.

*Gas metal arc welding (MIG welding)*

This uses a consumable wire electrode fed through a welding gun, with an inert gas shielding the weld area.

Advantages: High deposition rates and efficiency, good for welding thin materials.

Disadvantages: Sensitive to wind and drafts in outdoor applications.

*Gas tungsten arc welding (TIG welding)*

This utilises a non-consumable tungsten electrode, a filler metal (if needed), and an inert gas for shielding.

Advantages: Provides high-quality, clean welds, suitable for thin materials and non-ferrous metals.

Disadvantages: Slower process compared to others, requires high skill levels.

*Stick welding (Electroslag welding)*

A consumable electrode is fed continuously into the weld zone, creating a molten pool that solidifies into a joint.

Advantages: High deposition rates, efficient for thick materials.

Disadvantages: Limited joint configurations, lower productivity compared to some processes.

*Resistance spot welding*

This joins two or more metal sheets by applying heat and pressure at localised points using copper electrodes.

Advantages: Fast and efficient for mass production, creates consistent and repeatable welds.

Disadvantages: Limited to specific joint configurations, not suitable for thick materials.

*Oxy-acetylene welding*

This uses a gas flame produced by burning oxygen and acetylene to melt and join metals.

Advantages: Portable and versatile, applicable to various materials.

Disadvantages: Slower compared to some other processes, limited to ferrous metals.

**Cutting** methods and equipment include thermal cutting (plasma, laser, oxy-fuel), and abrasive cutting (water jet, abrasive discs).

Advantages: Precision cutting is possible with advanced methods, suitable for a wide range of materials.

Disadvantages: Some methods may produce heat-affected zones, advanced equipment can be expensive.

**Brazing** is a process of joining metals using a filler metal that melts above 450°C but below the melting point of the base metals. The filler metal is drawn into the joint by capillary action (liquid flowing in a narrow tube or cylinder). Typically used for joining metals like copper, brass, and steel.

Advantages: Strong, durable joints, suitable for dissimilar metals, can join thin-walled sections.

Disadvantages: Requires careful preparation and cleaning, lower joint strength compared to welding.

**Soldering** is similar to brazing but with a lower melting point (below 450°C). Soldering joins metals using a filler metal that melts and flows into the joint. Commonly used for plumbing to join copper pipes. Other materials it can be used on include brass and iron.

Advantages: Low melting point avoids damage to heat-sensitive components, useful for joining electrical components, creates neat, clean joints.

Disadvantages: Joints may not be as strong as brazed or welded joints, limited to materials with low melting points.

**Flame cutting**, often referred to as oxy-fuel cutting, uses a combination of oxygen and a fuel gas (acetylene, propane) to melt and remove metal. Commonly used for cutting carbon steel.

Advantages: Suitable for thick sections, portable and versatile, inexpensive equipment.

Disadvantages: Limited to ferrous metals, slower than some modern cutting methods, heat-affected zone in the cut which can reduce strength or cause corrosion.

**Thermal lancing** involves burning a steel tube filled with a mixture of iron powder and a metal tube that serves as a fuel, producing intense heat to cut through materials. Primarily used for cutting and piercing thick metals.

Advantages: Effective for cutting thick sections, versatile for demolition and industrial applications.

Disadvantages: Limited precision, consumes significant amounts of oxygen.

**Angle grinders** use a rapidly rotating abrasive disc to grind, cut, or polish materials. They come in various sizes and can be handheld or stationary. Suitable for cutting and grinding metal, stone, concrete, and more. This functionality also brings with it the potential for heat generation, sparks, and fire hazards. An angle grinder smoothing rough surfaces or sharpening blades can lead to the creation of fine particles, posing risks of dust ignition or sparks.

Advantages: Versatile for various applications, portable and easy to use, inexpensive compared to some alternatives.

Disadvantages: Generates sparks and dust, requires proper safety precautions.

**Hot air guns** use electric or gas-powered heating elements to produce a stream of hot air. They are commonly used for softening materials, paint removal, or plastic welding.

Advantages: Precise control of temperature, suitable for heat-sensitive materials, portable and easy to use.

Disadvantages: Limited to lower-temperature applications, may require additional safety precautions.

## Understanding the Hot-Works Permit

The hot-works permit is an official authorisation granted by a Competent Person (someone qualified, experienced and aware of the risks involved with hot works), allowing specific hazardous tasks involving open flames, intense heat, or sparks. This permit serves as a comprehensive safety blueprint, ensuring that necessary precautions are implemented to mitigate risks of fire and explosions. The permit must be documented, authorised and monitored.

## Key Elements of a Hot-Works Permit

The essential components of a hot-works permit are:

- Task description: Clearly outline the task to be executed, including details about the equipment, materials, and the location of the work.
- Safety precautions and procedures: Enumerate the safety measures and protocols that must be followed, such as adequate ventilation, fire prevention strategies, and the requirement for protective equipment.
- Authorised personnel: Specify the names and qualifications of the individuals permitted to conduct the hot work. Detail their roles and responsibilities in the process.
- Time frame: Define the period during which the permit is valid, ensuring that the task is limited to the specified

duration to minimise exposure to hazards (any extensions to time frames must be authorised by the permit issuer, upon checking the environment again prior to agreement).

- Fire watch and emergency response: Assign personnel responsible for monitoring the work area for potential fire risks. Outline the steps to be taken in case of emergencies.
- Equipment inspection: Establish the necessity for inspecting equipment before and after the task, guaranteeing that all machinery is in proper working condition.

**The Importance of the Hot-Works Permit**

As we consider the significance of the hot-works permit, several key points come to the fore:

- Risk management: The permit functions as an organised tool for managing risks, ensuring that potential hazards associated with hot work are identified and effectively addressed.
- Responsibility: By specifying authorised personnel and their responsibilities, the permit holds individuals accountable for adhering to safety procedures.
- Effective communication: The permit facilitates transparent communication among all parties involved, ensuring that everyone is well informed about the task, its associated risks, and the safety measures in place. The people involved in doing the job must sign the permit to show they understand the risks and the precautions necessary to mitigate the risks.
- Emergency readiness: Through provisions for fire watches and emergency response, the permit enhances the preparedness of workers to promptly address unforeseen incidents.

- Regulatory compliance: The issuance and adherence to a hot-works permit align with regulatory safety standards, mitigating potential legal liabilities and consequences.

## Risk Management for Heat Work

As well as the general risk management noted earlier in the book, there are some specific steps that should be taken when hot works are being carried out. Contractors should implement the following, which is in line with standard regulatory requirements.

### Hazard Identification

Identify potential hazards related to heat work, such as exposure to high temperatures, fire risks, or the release of hazardous substances.

### Training

Receive appropriate training on heat work, including the safe use of equipment, fire prevention, and the use of PPE.

### Risk Assessment

Thoroughly evaluate the workspace to identify potential hazards, including flammable materials, combustible surroundings, and ventilation issues.

### Isolation and Preparation

Isolate the workspace, preventing unauthorised access. Implement fire-resistant screens to contain sparks and designate fire watchers to maintain vigilance.

### PPE

Outfit personnel with appropriate PPE, including flame-resistant clothing, eye protection, and respiratory equipment.

### Fire Prevention

Equip the workspace with fire extinguishers and establish fire prevention measures, such as removing flammable materials from the vicinity. What cannot be removed, must be covered with a fire resistant material.

**Safe Working Distance**

Maintain a safe distance between the hot work and potentially flammable materials, structures, or equipment.

**Emergency Response**

Have a clear plan for emergency response, including extinguishing fires and evacuating personnel if necessary.

**Control Measures**

Implement control measures such as proper ventilation, the use of fire-resistant materials, and the availability of fire extinguishers or suppression systems to mitigate the risks associated with heat work.

**After Work Checks**

The area where the hot work was carried out must be checked again a few hours later, and before the contractors leave the site. Smouldering particles can take some time to progress into a fire, so it is imperative that the area is thoroughly checked for these before the site is left.

Whilst the use of heat has the strictest regulations, the preferred alternative is a non-heat method (cold cutting), and only to use heat if absolutely necessary. Stringent risk management strategies can reduce the likelihood of incidents or accidents, but it cannot eradicate the risk entirely, and has been the cause of substantial fires and large losses.

# Work at Height

Contracts often involve working at elevated levels, such as when installing roof trusses or constructing upper floors. Without proper fall protection measures, workers can be at risk of serious injuries or fatalities from falls. Work at height requires careful planning, training, and stringent adherence to safety protocols. Let's explore the intricacies of work at height, including the hazards, the various methods of access, fall minimisation strategies, and available training.

**Defining Work at Height: Beyond Ground Level**

Work at height encompasses activities performed above ground level, where there exists a risk of falling that could cause injury or damage. These tasks can range from minor elevation to significant altitudes, such as working on scaffolds, ladders, platforms, or rooftops.

**What are the main hazards of work at height?**

There are three main hazards associated with work at height, namely:

- Injuries and fatalities of workers - Either caused by falling from height, or objects falling from height.
- Damage to materials and plant - Again, either caused by falling from height, or objects falling on them from height.
- Third party injuries - Caused by objects falling from height, or injuries from unguarded height methods e.g. exposed scaffolding poles.

**Wind loading** is a significant consideration for construction activities involving work at height. Wind loading refers to the force exerted by the wind on structures, equipment, and workers, which can pose various hazards during construction projects. This force can vary based on wind speed, direction, and the surface area of the object or structure being impacted.

High winds can cause instability, sway, or even structural failure in scaffolding and other elevated work platforms which poses a risk to workers and the public. Wind can affect the safe operation of cranes, causing loads to swing uncontrollably or the crane itself to become unstable.

Strong gusts of wind can impact worker safety, knocking them off balance, increasing the risk of falls. Loose materials and tools can be picked up by the wind, becoming hazardous projectiles. Large but relatively light materials, such as boards or timber frames, can be blown by the wind and knock over workers, causing serious injuries even if they do not fall from height. High winds can halt work at height, leading to project delays and increased costs.

The risk management required for this particular hazard includes:

- Wind load calculations to determine the wind load that structures can safely withstand.
- Regular monitoring of weather forecasts and wind speeds to anticipate and plan for high wind conditions.
- Use of tie-downs, anchors, and braces to stabilise scaffolding and temporary structures.
- Implementing policies to suspend work at height when wind speeds exceed safe thresholds (cited by the HSE as speeds over 23mph).

- Ensuring all tools, materials, and equipment are securely fastened or stored when not in use.
- Training workers to recognise wind-related hazards and follow safety protocols.
- Establishing and practicing emergency procedures for high wind scenarios.

- Using guardrails and safety nets to provide additional protection.

## Methods of Work at Height: From Ladders to Rope Access

Multiple methods exist for work at height, each catering to specific tasks and environments. These include using ladders, scaffolds, mobile elevated work platforms (MEWPs), and even abseiling or rope access techniques for challenging locations.

### Ladders

The HSE provides guidance on the safe use of various types of ladders, which covers:

- Selection of the right type of ladder (considering height, weight capacity, and material)
- Ladder inspections prior to use
- Setting up and positioning the ladder correctly
- Climbing and descending safely and avoiding overreaching
- Where ladders should be used, and limiting use for extended periods or in hazardous conditions.
- Working load limits
- Regular maintenance
- Training and supervision

### Access stilts

These are adjustable-height devices worn by workers to elevate themselves without the need for ladders or scaffolding. These stilts typically consist of a footplate where the user's feet are strapped in, adjustable legs, and a base that provides stability.

Access stilts are particularly useful for plasterers and dry liners, and painters and decorators, who need to work on ceilings or high walls. These professionals use stilts to maintain mobility and work at elevated heights without repeatedly moving ladders or erecting scaffolding.

Using access stilts requires balance, coordination, and practice. Workers must be adept at walking and manoeuvring on stilts while carrying tools and materials. Proper training helps ensure safe and efficient use. CITB (Construction Industry Training Board) provides training on the safe use of access stilts.

The hazards include falls, obstacles and uneven surfaces leading to trips and falls.

Risk management must encompass the use of PPE including helmets, gloves, and knee pads. Workplace preparation must be carried out to keep the workspace clean and free of obstacles and to ensure surfaces are even and stable. Stilts must be regularly inspected for wear and tear, ensuring all components are in good working condition.

There may be implementation of a buddy system where workers using stilts are monitored by colleagues who can assist in case of an imbalance or fall.

There must be limits set for the amount of time spent on stilts to prevent fatigue or falls, and regular breaks must be taken.

**Scaffolding Types**

Scaffolding is a method used that is familiar to most, as we often have to navigate under these walkways on the street. Most people, however, do not know the numerous different types that can be used. Variations include:

*Single Scaffolding,* also known as bricklayers scaffolding due to its common use, is employed for tasks like bricklaying or rendering walls. This structure consists of elements that make its simplicity and adaptability make it a go-to choice for various projects, providing a stable platform for workers and materials.

*Tower Scaffolding* is erected vertically and is used for providing a stable platform at tall heights, and it's particularly suitable for tasks requiring access to multiple levels. Its mobility and ease of assembly make it ideal for short-term projects, where its height can be adjusted as needed.

*Trestle Scaffolding* comes into play when the ground is uneven or stairwells obstruct standard scaffold structures. It's highly portable, making it useful for tasks that require elevation and stability in challenging terrains. It is most commonly used for work inside rooms, such as for painting or repairs, up to a height of 5 metres.

*Mobile Scaffolding,* also known as rolling scaffolding, is designed for mobility. Fitted with wheels or casters, it allows workers to move the scaffold to different locations with ease. This adaptability is particularly beneficial for tasks that demand frequent repositioning.

*Suspended Scaffolding* is used when ground-based scaffolding isn't feasible. It's used for exterior maintenance, painting, or repairs on tall buildings. Suspended by ropes or cables, workers can access various heights while maintaining stability and safety.

**Choosing the Right Scaffold for the Task**

Selecting the appropriate scaffold depends on factors like project scope, duration, and site conditions. Each scaffold type is designed to cater to specific needs, ensuring that workers can operate efficiently and safely at various heights.

**Fall Minimisation Strategies for Scaffolding: Anchoring Safety**

Regardless of the method used, mitigating falls is paramount. Methods used for scaffolding are guardrails and toe boards, also referred to as edge protection. Erecting guardrails around the scaffold's perimeter prevents accidental falls. Toe boards add an extra layer of protection by preventing tools or materials from falling. Safety harnesses and lanyards are advised by industry guidance for work over 4 metres, but are not to be used on mobile towers.

For tower scaffolding, incorporating guardrails and midrails at all open sides and ends of the tower scaffold prevents accidental falls. For mobile scaffolding, the use of locking casters, and ensuring the casters are locked before using the scaffold, prevents unintended movement and instability, reducing the likelihood of falls. Using harnesses with mobile scaffolding on wheels, especially while the scaffold is in motion, is not advisable. Mobile scaffolding is designed for easy movement and repositioning, which can create a dynamic and potentially unstable working environment. Attaching a worker's harness to a mobile scaffold while it's being moved can lead to hazards such as tipping, loss of balance, or entanglement. For trestle scaffolding, ensuring the trestles are stable and properly set up is vital. Also, using guardrails on platforms can minimise the risk of falls.

Workers using suspended scaffolding should be equipped with fall arrest devices like harnesses and lanyards, along with proper anchoring systems.

**MEWPs (Mobile Elevated Work Platforms)**

MEWPs, a hallmark of modern construction, offer flexibility and precision. Let's have a look at some of their types and common applications.

*Scissor lifts* are recognisable by their crisscrossing support mechanisms, which provide vertical movement and a stable platform. They're suitable for tasks like maintenance, installation, and construction, both indoors and outdoors.

*Cherry pickers (boom lifts)* have extendable arms (booms) that offer both vertical and horizontal movement. Cherry pickers are used for tasks that require outreach, such as trimming trees, exterior painting, and installation on tall structures.

*Telescopic boom lifts* are similar to cherry pickers in that they feature extendable arms. However, their design allows for greater reach and versatility, making them ideal for tasks in challenging or hard-to-reach areas.

*Articulating boom lifts* feature multiple sections that allow the boom varied movement, providing flexibility and the ability to navigate around or over obstacles. They're well-suited for tasks that require precision and manoeuvrability.

*Push-Around Vehicle (PAV)* is a type of MEWP that is designed to be manually propelled by the operator. Unlike self-propelled MEWPs that have their own built-in power source for movement, a PAV relies on the operator to push or move it to the desired location. PAVs are often compact and lightweight, making them suitable for tasks that require access to tight spaces or areas with limited manoeuvrability. They typically have a small platform that the operator stands on while working at height. PAVs are used for tasks such as maintenance, repairs, and installation in environments where a larger MEWP might be impractical or unnecessary.

**Safeguarding Heights: Fall Minimisation for MEWPs**
Workers operating MEWPs should wear a properly fitted harness and be securely attached to the MEWP's designated anchor points using a lanyard. This fall arrest system prevents workers from falling off the platform in case of sudden jolts or loss of balance. MEWPs are equipped with guardrails and toe boards around the platform. These prevent workers from accidentally stepping off the edge. A fully enclosed platform minimises the risk of falls and provides a secure working environment.

**What factors need to be considered when choosing the correct MEWP for the job?**

Choosing the best MEWP for a specific job requires a thoughtful and strategic approach. Considerations range from the task's nature to the environment's challenges.

*Understanding the task*

Determining the required reach and access. Do they need vertical, horizontal, or both types of movement?

*Assessing the environment*

Is it indoor or outdoor? Are there obstacles, tight spaces, or uneven terrain? Are there any overhead obstacles such as power lines or structures that could hinder movement?

*Evaluating height and reach*

What is the required working height? MEWPs come with different reach capabilities, so one must be chosen that reaches the height they need to access. If horizontal reach is crucial, boom-type MEWPs that offer extension must be considered.

*Platform capacity*

What are the estimated number of workers and the amount of equipment/materials that will be on the platform? A MEWP with adequate load capacity must be chosen.

*Machine dimensions*

Does the MEWP dimensions allow easy access to the work area? A MEWP that is too large might not fit in tight spaces.

*Power source*

Should it be electric, diesel or hybrid? A choice must be made between different power sources based on the work environment and power availability. Electric MEWPs are quieter and emission-free, making them suitable for indoor use.

*Stability and ground conditions*

Considering the ground conditions where the MEWP will be positioned is vital. Uneven or sloping surfaces might require special stabilisation features.

*Operator competence*

Does the operator have the necessary training and qualifications to operate the chosen type of MEWP?

If uncertain about the correct type to use, contractors consult with experts who specialise in MEWP operations. They can provide valuable insights based on their experience.

## How do these choices positively impact risk control when using MEWPs?

- Adhering to load capacity guidelines is crucial to avoid toppling.
- Keeping the MEWP away from potential hazards such as overhead obstructions, power lines, or uneven surfaces that could otherwise compromise stability.
- Operating in a clear and hazard-free environment minimises the risk of accidents.
- MEWPs should be positioned on level ground to maintain stability. Sloping surfaces can affect the machine's balance and stability.
- Checking ground conditions before setting up the MEWP is essential for safe operation.
- Operators should continuously monitor their surroundings, the machine's stability, and any changes in conditions, and must therefore be competent to do so.
- Immediate action must be taken in cases of unforeseen situations that could lead to falls.

**Rope Access Techniques**

These methods represent a specialised and versatile approach to work at height, where conventional methods may prove impractical or unsafe. This method involves skilled technicians using ropes, harnesses, and anchoring systems to access elevated locations. Rope access techniques come into play for intricate tasks and challenging locations.

Fall minimisation methods used include:

- Double rope system: Technicians use two separate ropes - a working rope and a backup rope - providing redundancy in case of primary rope failure.
- Fall arrest devices: Personal protective equipment, such as descenders and ascenders, allow workers to control their descent and ascent while arresting falls.
- Harness and attachment points: Workers wear specialised harnesses with multiple attachment points for ropes, tools, and equipment. This distributes the load and prevents discomfort during prolonged work.

Rope access techniques excel in scenarios where traditional methods prove challenging:

- *Structural inspection and maintenance:* Rope access is ideal for inspecting and maintaining tall buildings, bridges, and structures where scaffolding or other platforms are impractical.
- *High-risk environments:* In hazardous locations like cliffs, oil rigs, and industrial chimneys, rope access offers safe access for repair and maintenance.
- *Confined spaces:* Rope access can navigate confined spaces where setting up scaffolding or other equipment is difficult.

- *Installation and surveying:* Tasks like installing signage, capturing aerial photography, and conducting surveys benefit from rope access's agility.

**Selecting the Right Method: Tailoring to Task and Terrain**
Choosing the appropriate method depends on the task's complexity, duration, and location. Scaffolding is versatile for longer projects, while MEWPs and rope access techniques cater to varying challenges.

**Promoting Safety through Adherence**
While stringent fall minimisation methods can greatly minimise fall risks, proper training, use of appropriate personal protective equipment (PPE), regular inspection of equipment, and comprehensive risk assessments are paramount. Workers should be educated on fall hazards and trained to react appropriately in emergency situations.

Harnesses are intended to provide fall protection and should be used in situations where the worker needs to remain stationary or secured in a particular location. When working on mobile scaffolding, fall protection methods like guardrails, toe boards, and proper access control are more suitable for preventing falls and ensuring worker safety during movement.

It's important that workers always follow manufacturer guidelines, industry best practices, and proper training when using any fall protection equipment or working at height.

# Training and Experience
The area of work at height demands expertise and hazard awareness is key. Adequate training is crucial, covering areas like hazard recognition, proper equipment usage and maintenance, and emergency procedures. Acquiring certifications such as PASMA

(Prefabricated Access Suppliers' and Manufacturers' Association) and LOLER (Lifting Operations and Lifting Equipment Regulations) ensures compliance and proficiency. MEWP operators require IPAF (International Powered Access Federation) training. Rope access demands skilled personnel with certifications from IRATA (Industrial Rope Access Trade Association). These certifications are discussed in more detail below.

For scaffolding, CISRS (Construction Industry Scaffolders Record Scheme) qualifications are vital. Scaffold erectors are specialists in constructing and dismantling scaffolds—a pivotal element in work at height. Their role extends beyond structure assembly; they meticulously ensure the scaffold's stability, load-bearing capacity, and continuing adherence to safety standards.

## Work at Height Accreditations

Accreditations ensure that individuals are competent in the specific techniques and equipment used for working at height. Proper training contributes to a safer working environment, reducing the risk of falls and accidents and adherence to industry-specific regulations and standards is essential for legal compliance and best practices in working at height.

## PASMA (Prefabricated Access Suppliers' and Manufacturers' Association)

PASMA is a trade association that focuses on the safe use of mobile access towers. PASMA provides training, guidance, and standards for the use, inspection, and assembly of mobile access towers, which are commonly used in construction and other industries for working at height.

PASMA Training:

- Covers the correct methods for assembling and dismantling mobile access towers to ensure stability and safety.

- Participants learn about the safe use of towers, including inspection procedures to identify and rectify potential issues.
- Training complies with industry standards and regulations related to working at height.

Benefits:
- PASMA training ensures that individuals are competent in the assembly, use, and inspection of mobile access towers.
- Proper training contributes to a safer working environment, reducing the risk of accidents when working at height.
- PASMA certification aligns with industry standards and regulations, demonstrating compliance with best practices.

## LOLER (Lifting Operations and Lifting Equipment Regulations)

LOLER is a set of regulations that specifically address the safe use of lifting equipment, including equipment used for work at height. LOLER applies to a wide range of lifting equipment, from cranes to simple pulley systems, and it includes provisions for the regular inspection and maintenance of such equipment.

Key Components:
- LOLER requires the thorough examination of lifting equipment by competent individuals at specified intervals.
- Lifting equipment must be accompanied by a valid certificate of thorough examination, and records of examinations must be maintained.

Benefits:
- LOLER ensures that lifting equipment used for work at height is safe, properly maintained, and regularly inspected.
- Compliance with LOLER is a legal requirement, and adherence to the regulations helps avoid legal consequences and ensures a safe working environment.

**IPAF (International Powered Access Federation)**

IPAF is an international organisation that focuses on the safe and effective use of powered access equipment, including MEWPs and aerial work platforms (AWPs). IPAF provides training and promotes best practices for working at height with powered access equipment.

IPAF Training:

- Training covers the safe operation of MEWPs, including scissor lifts and boom lifts.
- Participants learn about safety guidelines, risk assessments, and emergency procedures when working with powered access equipment.
- IPAF training aligns with relevant industry regulations and standards to ensure compliance.

Benefits:

- IPAF training ensures that operators are competent in the safe use of powered access equipment.
- IPAF certification is globally recognised, making it valuable for individuals working internationally.

- IPAF promotes a safety culture by providing guidelines and best practices for working at height with powered access equipment.

**IRATA (Industrial Rope Access Trade Association)**

IRATA provides training and certification for individuals using rope access techniques for work at height in various industries.

**CISRS (Construction Industry Scaffolders Record Scheme)**

CISRS is a scaffolding industry scheme in the UK that provides training and certification for scaffolders, ensuring safe working at height.

# RAMS for Work at Height

Work at height requires meticulous planning. Risk Assessments and Method Statements (RAMS) are indispensable tools, outlining potential hazards, control measures, and emergency protocols specific to each task. These documents facilitate safety planning and communication among the workforce.

A comprehensive risk assessment is a systematic process, and when applied to work at height:

- It pinpoints potential hazards like falls, instability, equipment malfunctions, and environmental factors specific to the work at height task.
- It evaluates the likelihood of each hazard occurring and the severity of its potential impact, and the assessment quantifies the risk levels involved.
- Based on the risk levels, appropriate control measures are determined. These could include using fall protection equipment, implementing work procedures, or choosing a different access method.
- The risk assessment outlines emergency response plans in case of accidents or unforeseen events during work at height.

A method statement outlines the precise steps, procedures, and precautions for performing a specific task safely. For work at height, a method statement:

- *Defines the task:* It describes the work at height task in detail, including the purpose, scope, and sequence of actions.
- *Enumerates equipment:* The method statement lists the equipment, tools, and personal protective gear required for the task.

- *Specifies procedures:* It lays out step-by-step procedures for setting up equipment, ascending to the work area, performing the task, and descending safely.
- *Addresses contingencies:* Contingency plans are outlined, detailing how to respond to unforeseen challenges or changes in conditions.
- *Highlights personnel responsibilities:* The roles and responsibilities of each team member involved in the task are clearly defined.

RAMS are tailored to the specific work at height task, accounting for its unique challenges, environment, and equipment.

## Falls from Height

According to the relevant professional bodies, over 75% of falls from height are caused by low falls – two metres or less. This is from stepladders/ladders being used incorrectly, or overstretching, or using equipment not intended for work at height, such as benches or chairs. In addition, the most common heights where fatalities occur is from zero to six metres, followed by six to 12 metres. Falls from height over 15m seem to be less common, usually because there are stricter controls in place, such as fall arrest equipment, edge protection, and the necessary and stringent training and qualifications required to use the equipment required to reach these heights.

# Work at Depth

Work at depth demands specialised skills, vigilant safety measures, and meticulous planning. Let's explore the nuances of work at depth, its applications, safety considerations, methods, and the imperative role of safeguarding underground services.

Work at depth encapsulates activities carried out below ground level, encompassing tunnels, excavations, and confined spaces (this is covered in more detail in the next section). It caters to tasks that require skilful execution in an environment where challenges are as intricate as they are diverse.

The applications are vast - ranging from tunnel construction and maintenance to plumbing, pipeline installation, and installation of cabling. Each demands a distinct set of skills and safety precautions. However in this section I will address work predominantly up to three metres depth.

## When is work at shallow depths necessary?

Work at shallow depths becomes relevant in scenarios where excavation, maintenance of underground systems, or repairs within confined spaces are required. While the depth might not be substantial, the hazards and safety concerns are still considerable. Tasks include:

- Laying pipelines or cables,
- Maintenance or installation of utilities such as water, gas or electrical systems,
- Maintenance or installation of drainage systems and underground structures,
- Excavations for foundations or footings*.

*Footings are horizontal structural elements that are typically made of concrete. They are located beneath the ground's surface and spread out beneath the walls or columns of a building. The primary purpose of footings is to distribute the weight of the structure evenly to the soil beneath, preventing settlement, sinking, or shifting.

**What depth?**

The depth at which underground cables and services are buried can vary depending on several factors, including local regulations, the type of utility, and the geographical location. There are no statutory depths as ground levels change over time. However, there are some general guidelines:

| Cable or Service | Typical depth |
|---|---|
| Electricity cables | 500mm to 900mm |
| Gas pipes | 600mm to 1200mm |
| Water pipes | 750mm to 1200mm * |
| Telecom. cables (fibre optic, telephone) | 300mm to 600mm ** |
| Sewer/drainage pipes | 600mm to several metres *** |

* Subject to frost protection requirements
** These cables are often shallower because they are less susceptible to damage from excavation activities.
*** Sewer and drainage pipes are buried at varying depths, depending on the local sewer system and topography.

It's important to note that these depths are general guidelines and can vary significantly depending on soil conditions, location (for example footpaths versus carriageways), climate, and utility provider preferences. HSE provides guidance on the precautionary steps to take, while National Joint Utilities Group/Street Works UK Ltd (the street works industry's representative body) provides more precise information regarding depth and colour coding of the various utilities in different locations.

## What are the main hazards with work at depth?
A significant hazard to be aware of is damage to underground services, where workers are not aware of the depth or positioning of the utilities and strike a cable. This could result in the loss of electricity to the surrounding neighbourhood, or damage to surrounding property if a water pipe was punctured and significant amounts of water were released into the air.

Injuries to workers can occur from:
- falls into the excavated area,
- collapse or caving in of the excavation or trench whilst working within the excavation area,
- being trapped inside plant such as a digger when it loses its stability, then tilts and falls into the excavation site.

Injuries to third parties can occur from falling into excavation areas that have not been secured, cordoned off, or clearly signposted. Damage to plant can occur if it falls into the excavated area, either whilst being operated or where it is left unattended on an unstable surface, allowing it to slide and fall. It could also be damaged if the excavation area caves in, and the plant is situated at depth.

## Identifying the Location of Underground Services
When conducting excavation or construction work near underground services, it's crucial to verify the depth and location of utilities through utility detection and mapping services and to comply with local regulations and best practices to prevent damage and ensure safety. Damaging utilities like water, gas, electricity, or telecommunications can lead to accidents, service disruptions, and costly repairs.

The Pipelines Safety Regulations 1996 mandate certain safety measures for pipelines. However, the specific depth requirements for underground pipelines are not specified. To determine the precise depth requirements for pipelines and underground services in the area, the following sources are consulted by contractors:

- Health and Safety Executive (HSE): The HSE provides comprehensive guidance on safety requirements for construction, excavation, and work involving underground services. You can access their guidelines and resources on the official HSE website for further information.

- Utility providers: Utility companies responsible for the pipelines and services within any area often have specific guidelines and requirements regarding the depth at which their services should be buried. Contractors contact these providers directly or refer to their documentation which can provide valuable insights into depth requirements.

- Local Authorities: Local authorities may also have regulations or bylaws that govern construction and excavation activities, including depth requirements for underground services. Contractors check with local authority for specific requirements in the area.

**Utility detection** is a critical process in construction and excavation projects to locate and map underground utilities. Several types of scanning technologies and equipment are used for utility detection, known as Cable Avoidance Tools (CAT), a few examples of these are:

- Ground Penetrating Radar (GPR)

GPR is one of the most common and versatile tools for utility detection. It uses radar pulses to create an image of subsurface objects and structures. GPR systems typically consist of a control unit and a handheld antenna or ground-coupled antenna. GPR can detect various types of utilities and provide depth information.

- Electromagnetic Locators (EM)

Electromagnetic locators use electromagnetic fields to detect conductive materials like metal pipes and cables. These devices are handheld and consist of a transmitter and receiver. They are particularly useful for locating metallic utilities.

- Acoustic Pipe Locators

These devices are used primarily for locating non-metallic water and sewer pipes. They work by listening for the sound of flowing water through the pipes. Acoustic pipe locators are often used in conjunction with ground markings or utility maps.

The choice of utility detection equipment depends on various factors, including the type of utilities to be located, the depth of the utilities, the composition of the soil, and the project's specific requirements. Often, a combination of technologies may be used to ensure accurate utility detection and mapping. It's also essential to have trained personnel who can operate and interpret the data from these devices effectively.

**Once the Utilities have been Detected**
It's essential to follow a series of steps to ensure the safety of workers and the integrity of the utilities. Here's a summary of what needs to be done:
*Documenting the findings*
Contractors record the location and depth of detected utilities accurately on site plans or drawings. The ground or pavement surface is clearly marked to indicate the presence and path of utilities. There is national colour coding that have been agreed by most utilities, this can be found in more detail within Streetworks UK '*Guidelines on the positioning and colour coding of*

*underground utilities' apparatus'.* This should be understood by all those working on the site.

*Verifying the information*

Cross-verify the detected utilities with existing utility maps, as-built drawings, or records from utility companies to ensure accuracy.

*Assessing risks*

Evaluate potential risks related to these utilities.

*Notifying relevant parties*

Inform utility companies and authorities about detected utilities.

*Adjusting plans*

Modify construction plans if needed to avoid utility damage.

*Implementing safety measures*

Establish safety protocols, train workers, and protect utilities during work.

*Utility relocation or protection*

If utility relocation is necessary, coordinate with utility companies to safely move or reroute the utilities. This may require permits and specialised equipment. In cases where relocation is not feasible, implement protective measures such as shoring, casing, or sleeving to prevent damage to the utilities during construction.

*Regular monitoring*

Continuously check and monitor utility safety.

*Emergency response*

Develop and communicate emergency response plans.

*Inspect and document*

Regularly inspect and maintain detailed records including any incidents or near misses.

*Final verification*

Confirm utilities are undamaged after work completion.

Remember that working near utilities requires a high degree of caution and adherence to safety protocols. Proper planning, communication, and coordination with utility companies are crucial to a successful construction or excavation project in areas with underground utilities.

## Navigating Shallow Depths: Methods, Safety, and Risk Management

Working at depths from zero to three metres is common in construction and infrastructure projects, particularly when new foundations or maintenance is required. Despite the relatively shallow depth compared to other more complex or specialist contracts, it's vital to employ appropriate methods of access, ensure the prevention of collapses, and implement effective risk management strategies. Let's delve into these aspects.

### Methods of Access: Precision and Safety

Accessing work areas at shallow depths requires careful consideration of methods that balance efficiency and safety.
*Ramps and sloping:* For excavations or trenches, ramps and sloping can provide gradual access while minimising the risk of collapse. Proper angles and shoring are essential for stability.
*Steps and ladders:* For structures like manholes or inspection chambers, steps or ladders allow workers to descend safely. They should be well-maintained and secure.

### Prevention of Collapse: Ensuring Ground Stability

Preventing collapses in shallow-depth work is crucial for worker safety and project success.
*Shoring:* Temporary shoring systems like hydraulic or timber shoring provide lateral support to excavation walls, preventing them from caving in.

*Sloping:* Properly sloping the sides of excavations to a safe angle, as per regulations, reduces the risk of collapse.

*Trench boxes:* In trenching work, trench boxes are used to protect workers and prevent cave-ins. These are placed within the excavation to provide a protective enclosure. Trench boxes or shields are designed to withstand soil pressures and provide a protective barrier against collapses.

## Risk Management: Safeguarding Every Step

Robust risk management is fundamental to ensuring safety at depth, and contractors must carry out the following:

*Site/risk assessment*

Conduct a thorough site assessment to identify potential hazards and soil conditions. Different soils have varying levels of stability and pose different risks. Evaluate groundwater levels as they can affect excavation stability. High water tables may require dewatering or specialised shoring methods.

*Safety training and competence*

Ensure all workers involved in work at depth are trained and competent in safe excavation and access procedures, and the use of safety equipment. Assign experienced supervisors to oversee work at depth and make critical safety decisions.

*Safety barriers*

Use safety barriers, fencing, or barricades to restrict unauthorised access to excavation areas. Clearly post signage indicating the presence of an excavation and the associated risks. Include emergency contact information.

*Ventilation and hazard monitoring*

Continuously monitor excavation conditions, soil stability, potential gas hazards, and weather factors that could affect safety.

*Control measures*

Contractors should implement control measures to manage the risks associated with work at depth, such as the use of personal protective equipment, and the buddy system for monitoring and assistance.

*Daily inspections*

Conduct daily inspections of excavation sites, shoring systems, and safety equipment before work begins.

*Emergency response and rescue planning*

Develop an emergency response plan that includes procedures for evacuation and rescue in case of accidents or collapses. Ensure that necessary rescue equipment, such as retrieval systems and harnesses, is readily available and maintained.

*Documentation and incident reporting*

Maintain detailed records of site assessments, safety training, inspections, and emergency drills. Establish a clear process for reporting incidents, near misses, and safety concerns, and ensure it is followed consistently.

*Compliance with Regulations*

Ensure full compliance with local, regional, and national regulations related to excavation and work at depth.

## Safe Excavation Practices

*Hand digging:* Whenever feasible, contractors commence with hand digging. This approach allows for precise excavation around known or suspected utilities, minimising the risk of damage.

*Non-destructive digging (NDD):* Contractors may choose to deploy NDD equipment, such as vacuum excavation systems, to reduce the potential for utility damage.

**Training**

While there aren't specific qualifications solely for work at depth outside of confined spaces, certain industry-specific qualifications and training programs can be relevant, especially when working near or with underground services, excavations, or other situations involving depths. These qualifications include:

- CITB Site Safety Plus Courses: The Construction Industry Training Board (CITB) offers various safety courses, such as the Site Management Safety Training Scheme (SMSTS) and Site Supervisor Safety Training Scheme (SSSTS), which cover safety aspects, including working around excavations and underground services.
- NRSWA (New Roads and Street Works Act) Qualifications: These qualifications are essential for anyone involved in street works or excavation work, such as utility workers. They cover safe excavation practices and working near underground services.
- Construction Plant Competence Scheme (CPCS): CPCS offers training and certification for plant operators, including those who operate equipment for excavation and groundwork, such as diggers and dumper trucks.
- NVQs (National Vocational Qualifications): These are work-based qualifications in various construction-related roles, including groundwork and excavation. They can provide practical knowledge of safe work practices related to excavation.
- Utility industry qualifications: Specific utility companies often provide training and qualifications for their employees and contractors who work with underground services, ensuring they understand the unique risks and safety measures associated with these environments.

- City & Guilds Certifications: City & Guilds offers various construction-related qualifications that cover safety practices and skills relevant to excavation and groundwork.
- HSE (Health and Safety Executive) Courses: The HSE provides various training and guidance materials related to excavation and safety, which can be useful for individuals and organisations involved in work at depth.

It's important to note that when working at depths, particularly in excavation and groundwork, compliance with Health and Safety regulations, including the Construction (Design and Management) Regulations 2015 (CDM Regulations), is crucial. Employers should ensure that their workers receive the necessary training and have the knowledge required to perform their tasks safely. Training providers and industry organisations often offer guidance on the most appropriate qualifications for specific roles and tasks involving work at depth.

# Confined Spaces

## Understanding Hazards

A confined space is defined as a limited-access area large enough for a person to enter and work but not designed for continuous occupation. These spaces often have restricted entry and exit points and can include tanks, silos, tunnels, sewers, and storage bins. Working in confined spaces poses unique challenges and hazards that require careful risk management.

The various hazards presented include:

- Limited oxygen: Reduced oxygen levels can lead to asphyxiation, making it difficult to breathe.
- Toxic Atmospheres: The presence of harmful gases or chemicals can cause poisoning and severe health issues.
- Flammable substances: Gases or substances that ignite easily can lead to fires or explosions.
- Engulfment: Workers can be trapped or engulfed by loose materials, liquids, or flowing solids.
- Physical constraints: Confined spaces often have cramped quarters, making movement difficult and increasing the risk of injury.

## Risk Management

Working in confined spaces necessitates a stringent approach to risk management to mitigate potential hazards effectively. Here is a summary of the protocols in line with the Confined Spaces Regulations 1997, which states the work may only be undertaken with a safe system of work in place, and only then if doing the work in the confined space cannot be avoided.

*Identification and assessment*

Identify confined spaces in the workplace and assess the risks associated with each. Determine if entry is necessary; if not, consider alternative work methods.

*Training and competence*

Ensure workers receive proper training for confined space entry. Verify workers' competence in recognising hazards, using safety equipment, and following emergency procedures.

*Safe entry procedures*

Develop meticulous entry procedures, including permits for confined space work. Use gas detectors to monitor air quality within the confined space continuously.

*Ventilation*

Implement effective ventilation systems to maintain safe oxygen levels and eliminate harmful gases from confined spaces.

*Valves locked shut*

Ensure that all valves controlling the flow of substances into and out of confined spaces are securely locked shut to prevent accidental activation. This is part of what is known as lockout/tagout (LOTO), which is a safety procedure to prevent the release of hazardous energy sources (such as electrical, mechanical, hydraulic, pneumatic, chemical, thermal, or other forms of energy) while workers are servicing or maintaining them.

*Rescue plans*

Establish and record rescue plans and have appropriate rescue equipment readily available.

Train personnel in rescue procedures. Workers should not rely solely on the emergency services but should have procedures for summoning emergency services if required. Develop clear emergency procedures for incidents such as gas leaks or engulfment, clearly marking exit routes. Conduct regular drills to ensure workers understand and can execute emergency plans.

*Personal Protective Equipment (PPE)*
Provide workers with appropriate PPE, including respiratory protection, harnesses, and communication equipment. Appropriate breathing apparatus must be provided when necessary to protect against insufficient oxygen levels or the presence of toxic gases.
*Communication*
Maintain constant communication with workers inside confined spaces to relay important information instantly. Prohibit lone working in confined spaces. Always use the buddy system to ensure mutual safety and prompt assistance in emergencies.
*Continuous monitoring*
Continuously monitor conditions inside confined spaces during work. Evacuate workers immediately if conditions deteriorate beyond acceptable safety limits. Workers should not be complacent that if circumstances are safe one day, they will be safe the next.
*Record keeping*
Maintain comprehensive records of all confined space activities, including risk assessments, permits, training records, and incident reports.
*Review and improvement*
Regularly review confined space procedures and incidents to identify areas for improvement and implementing necessary changes.
Working in confined spaces demands rigorous planning, training, and adherence to safety protocols. Effective risk management is crucial to protect workers from the unique hazards associated with these environments.

# Work in Basements

## Hazards of Basement Work

Working in basements brings unique challenges and potential pitfalls that contractors must face, hazards that need to be identified and managed to reduce risk of injury to workers and damage to plant.

Basement projects can range from open sites as part of new build projects to retro fitting under existing buildings. This is particularly common in London, where space limitations have resulted in buildings being extended downwards to accommodate additional living or work space, and can be multiple storeys to maximise the potential within a demise and the value for investments.

Contractors involved in basement work have the potential to cause considerable problems both from a works and a liability perspective. Retro fit basements are higher risk for works compared to those as part of a new build property. The primary concern would be the potential collapse and loss of the works, temporary works and machinery being used at the time.

Here are some key points to consider for basement work:

- Basement work can adversely affect a building's structural stability. Contractors must exercise vigilance to ensure that their activities do not compromise the foundation's integrity or create vulnerabilities.

- The tight quarters of a basement can increase the likelihood of accidental property damage to the property under renovation. Contractors may inadvertently damage walls, floors, or utility systems, leading to costly repairs and potential liability claims.

- The restricted confines of basements pose logistical challenges when manoeuvring heavy machinery, potentially leading to accidental damage to equipment.
- Proper ventilation is crucial when using equipment in basements. Inadequate ventilation can lead to the build-up of harmful fumes or dust, potentially causing damage to equipment.
- The basement's confined nature, inadequate ventilation, and potential exposure to mould or asbestos heighten the risk of injuries among workers. Contractors must prioritise safety protocols and compliance with regulations.
- Basements often house electrical systems, water heaters, and other potential hazards.
- There would be the exposure to damage resulting from defective workmanship, materials etc. that could be expensive to rectify if the damage occurs towards the end of the project – the timing of the damage would have a significant impact on costs.
- Basements are vulnerable to flood damage including water run-off.
- Work in terraced properties is a negative feature due to the potential for larger losses compared to potential losses caused by damage in a detached property.

**Positive Features and Specific Risk Management**
There are some key factors that would be considered positive and lower risk in the assessment of basement work:
- A high level of competence of the contractor as basement contracts require specialist skillset.
- Use of a panel of proven expert sub-contractors they use repeatedly to ensure a consistency in the works undertaken

rather than a reliance upon the best tender price for specified works to be undertaken.

- Working to overall architect specification.

## Factors to Check and Evaluate

*Method of excavation used*

Excavation within basements uses various methods, including hand tools and machinery. Each method has its advantages and risks. Hand tools, whilst being cost-effective and suitable for smaller basement excavations or tight spaces, makes excavation slower and may extend project timelines. Machinery, such as excavators, backhoes and trenchers, are highly efficient and suitable for large basement excavations, but do have greater risk. These include injuries and fatalities if not operated by trained personnel (backhoes are particularly prone to tipping if not operated on stable ground), damage to underground utilities like water pipes or electrical cables, and trench collapses.

To mitigate these inherent risks, comprehensive safety measures must be in place during basement excavation, including:

- Proper training and certification for equipment operators.
- Adequate trench shoring and protective systems.
- Clear marking and identification of underground utilities.
- Regular maintenance and inspections of machinery.
- Personal protective equipment (PPE) for workers.
- Ventilation and air quality monitoring in confined spaces.

Safety should be a top priority when conducting basement excavations, and a thorough risk assessment and safety plan should be part of the project management process to ensure the well-being of all involved personnel.

*Experience of contractors*
Any sub contractors used must have experience in this very
specialised type of work – The main contractor must have a system
of vetting in place to check their capabilities and ensure they have
their own adequate insurances in place.

*Does the property already have piled foundations in place?*
This presents a unique set of risks and challenges. These risks
primarily revolve around the potential impact on the structural
integrity of the existing foundations, safety of workers, and the
stability of the excavation site. Here are the key risks associated
with excavation beneath or near piled foundations:

- Undermining the stability and integrity of the piled
  foundations - The excavation process can cause soil
  settlement, foundation movement, or soil erosion.
- Adjacent structure damage - Nearby structures or
  neighbouring buildings may be at risk of damage or
  settlement due to excavation activities near piled
  foundations. This can lead to disputes and potential liability
  issues.
- The proximity of piled foundations can increase the risk of
  trench collapses, endangering workers and further
  complicating the excavation process.

Risk management highlights:
- Comprehensive structural engineering assessment
- Implementation of shoring and underpinning techniques
- Careful planning and coordination
- Regular monitoring and inspections
- Adequate worker training and safety measures
- Compliance with local building codes, regulations, and
  permits for excavation

*Has the contract already started?*

Contracts that are already underway are unattractive to insurers as the exposure is higher as the contract progresses but the premium obtained will not be reflective of the risk.

*New build or retro fit?*

Whilst structural/excavation work in a basement is a major concern from an insurance perspective, internal fit outs of basements are not considered any higher risk than any other area of a building, nor a new build of a basement, as long as adequate controls and thorough risk management is in place.

# Work at Hazardous Locations

## Defining and Navigating Hazardous Locations

Embarking on projects within hazardous locations requires contractors to be well-versed in the complexities and risks associated with such environments.

Contractors often find themselves undertaking projects in environments where the potential for significant losses is elevated, necessitating specialised risk management considerations. Insurance companies consider various aspects when deciding whether a location is considered high risk/hazardous:

*Industry standards and regulations*

Insurance companies often refer to industry standards and regulations to assess the risk associated with certain locations. For example, facilities handling hazardous materials may be subject to regulations such as the Control of Major Accident Hazards (COMAH) regulations. Work at COMAH sites, or in close proximity to, is considered hazardous.

*Nature of operations*

The type of operations conducted at a location is a crucial factor. Industries with inherently high risks, such as chemical manufacturing, oil and gas, or transportation hubs, would be classified as hazardous.

*Environmental impact*

Locations with the potential for significant environmental impact may be considered hazardous. This can include sites near water bodies, ecologically sensitive areas, or locations where spills or releases could lead to environmental damage.

*Occupancy and Iinfrastructure*

The occupancy of a building or facility is considered. For instance, airports, railway stations, or large industrial complexes may be classified as hazardous due to the presence of large crowds, complex infrastructure, and potential for diverse risks.

*Historical loss data*

Insurance companies often analyse historical loss data to identify patterns and assess risk. Locations with a higher frequency or severity of past incidents may be classified as hazardous.

**The 'Hazardous' associated with 'Locations'**

Chemical exposure:

- Locations: Chemical plants, manufacturing facilities.
- Hazards: Exposure to hazardous substances, leading to health issues for workers and potential environmental contamination.

Fire and explosions:

- Locations: Chemical plants, refineries, fuel storage facilities.
- Hazards: The presence of flammable materials increases the likelihood of fires and explosions, causing significant property damage and potential loss of life.

Transportation risks:

- Locations: Airports, railways, shipping ports.
- Hazards: Accidents involving aircraft, trains, or ships can result in catastrophic consequences, including injuries, fatalities, and extremely costly damage to infrastructure.

Environmental impact:

- Locations: Areas near water bodies, ecologically sensitive zones.

- Hazards: Spills or releases of hazardous substances can lead to environmental damage, affecting ecosystems and water sources.

Structural failures:
- Locations: Large industrial complexes, manufacturing plants.
- Hazards: Structural failures in buildings or infrastructure can result in property damage, injuries, and business interruption.

Security threats:
- Locations: Airports, critical infrastructure sites.
- Hazards: The potential for terrorism, theft, or sabotage, leading to significant security and safety concerns.

Crowd management:
- Locations: Airports, stadiums, public transportation hubs.
- Hazards: Managing large crowds poses risks of stampedes, security breaches, and health and safety concerns.

**Additional Factors to Consider**
*Is it a one-off contract?*
For one-off contracts, workers will be less familiar with the specific hazards of the location. Rigorous site induction and comprehensive risk assessments are crucial to ensure their understanding of potential risks.
*Do they have previous experience?*
Prior experience with similar hazardous environments can be invaluable. Workers familiar with the intricacies of specific risks associated with, for example, chemical plants or railways, are better equipped to navigate and respond to potential hazards.

*Are they going to be working in areas of lower risk?*
Understanding whether the work is be conducted away from operational plant areas or high-risk processes can assist in assessing the exposure to severe hazards.

*Are they supervised?*
The level of supervision is critical, particularly for workers who may not be extensively experienced in hazardous environments, or those unfamiliar with the layout of the property. Where work is required within production or processing areas at a hazardous location, it is imperative that supervision is provided by the occupant of the building, to ensure that the workers stay within the safety zones and prevent any possible damage or injuries. Adequate supervision ensures that safety protocols are followed, and immediate responses can be activated in case of emergencies.

## Risk Management Measures

There are certain precautionary measures that are expected when undertaking work at hazardous locations.

*Comprehensive risk assessments*
Thorough assessments of potential hazards and risks specific to the location and operations.
Example measure: Regularly updated risk assessments with clear mitigation strategies.

*Emergency response plans*
Well-defined plans for responding to accidents, including fire response, evacuation procedures, and coordination with emergency services.
Example measure: Regular drills and testing of emergency response plans.

*Implementing safety protocols*
Establishing and enforcing stringent safety protocols is crucial.

Example measure: The use of personal protective equipment, adherence to established procedures, and regular safety procedure reviews to ensure they are still fit for purpose.

*Environmental controls*

Protocols to prevent and respond to environmental incidents, such as spills or releases.

Example measure: Use of containment systems, regular environmental impact assessments.

*Compliance with Regulations*

Adherence to relevant health and safety regulations, industry standards, and legal requirements.

Example measure: Regular audits to ensure compliance with regulatory standards.

*Safety training programs*

Ongoing safety training for employees, contractors, and relevant personnel.

Example measure: Certification programs, regular safety workshops, and training modules.

*Investment in preventive measures*

Proactive investment in preventive measures to reduce the likelihood of accidents.

Example measure: Regular maintenance of equipment, advice from external consultants regarding site specific risk assessments.

*Continuous improvement*

Hazardous environments are dynamic, and risks may evolve over time, therefore there must be a commitment to continuous improvement in safety measures based on incident reviews and industry best practices.

Example measure: Regularly updated safety protocols and procedures based on lessons learned.

# Work with Hazardous Substances

## Working with Hazardous Substances: A COSHH Perspective for Contractors

Undertaking projects involving hazardous substances requires contractors to consider the risks and safety considerations. Here we look at the definition of hazardous substances and examine the risks associated with these substances from a liability viewpoint. We will then explore the role of COSHH (Control of Substances Hazardous to Health) in ensuring workplace safety and look at other effective risk management strategies that contractors can use.

## Understanding the Hazards of Working with Hazardous Substances

Hazardous substances encompass a broad category of materials that, due to their nature, pose potential risks to human health and the environment. These substances can include chemicals, solvents, gases, and other materials with properties that may cause harm through inhalation, skin contact, or ingestion. In construction, exposure to such substances is a common concern, necessitating a proactive approach to safety.

Handling hazardous substances has several inherent risks. These may include acute or chronic health effects on workers, environmental damage, and potential legal consequences.

*Chemical exposure*

- Inhalation hazards: Inhalation of fumes, vapours, or dust from hazardous chemicals can lead to respiratory issues, irritation, or long-term health effects.
- Skin contact: Direct contact with hazardous substances can cause skin irritation, chemical burns, or allergic reactions.

*Toxicity and health effects*
- Acute toxicity: Some substances may have immediate toxic effects, leading to symptoms ranging from dizziness and nausea to more severe reactions.
- Chronic health effects: Prolonged exposure to certain substances may result in chronic health conditions, including respiratory disorders, organ damage, or cancer.

*Flammability and explosivity*
Certain hazardous substances are flammable or explosive, posing significant risks in the presence of ignition sources or incompatible materials.

*Chemical reactions*
Mixing incompatible substances can lead to chemical reactions, releasing toxic gases, heat, or other hazardous byproducts.

*Biological hazards*
Workers close to microorganisms or biological substances, such as in healthcare or research settings, face the risk of exposure to infectious agents and diseases.

*Exposure routes*
Ingesting hazardous substances accidentally, through contaminated hands or surfaces, can lead to poisoning and other health issues.

*Improper handling and storage*
- Spills and leaks: Accidental spills or leaks of hazardous substances can result in immediate exposure or environmental contamination.
- Incorrect storage: Inadequate storage of hazardous materials may lead to degradation, leakage, or uncontrolled reactions.

*Noise and vibration*
The use of equipment such as pumps, mixers, or machinery during the handling of hazardous substances can contribute to noise and vibration hazards.

*PPE challenges*
Improper use or failure to use PPE correctly may compromise its effectiveness in preventing exposure.

Considerations extend to ensuring that proper measures are in place to prevent exposure, providing adequate training, and complying with COSHH regulations. Failure to address these aspects may result in severe consequences for both the health of workers and the financial well-being of the contracting entity.

## COSHH Regulations

COSHH, or Control of Substances Hazardous to Health, is a set of regulations designed to protect workers from the risks associated with hazardous substances. Contractors working with such materials are obligated to assess and control these risks under COSHH. The regulations outline a systematic approach, emphasising the need to identify hazardous substances, assess the risks, implement control measures, and provide adequate information and training to workers.

## Risk Management Strategies Aligning with COSHH Principles

- Substitution and elimination: Where possible, contractors should substitute hazardous substances with less harmful alternatives or eliminate their use altogether.
- Engineering controls: Implementing engineering controls, such as ventilation systems or containment measures, helps minimise the release of hazardous substances into the workplace environment.
- Personal Protective Equipment (PPE): Provide workers with appropriate PPE, such as gloves, respirators, and eye protection, based on COSHH risk assessments. Training on the correct use and maintenance of PPE is crucial.

- Training and information: Equip workers with the knowledge and awareness required to handle hazardous substances safely. This includes understanding the potential risks, proper handling procedures, emergency response protocols, and the importance of hygiene practices.
- Emergency response planning: Develop and communicate emergency response plans for spills, leaks, or exposure incidents. Conduct regular drills to ensure a prompt and effective response.
- Regular monitoring and review: Continuously monitor the workplace for potential exposure and regularly review risk assessments and control measures. This ensures that strategies remain effective and relevant to evolving project conditions.
- Health monitoring: Establish regular health monitoring programs for workers exposed to hazardous substances. Include medical examinations to detect early signs of exposure-related health issues.
- COSHH compliance: Strict adherence to COSHH regulations is fundamental. This includes maintaining accurate records, conducting regular assessments, and promptly addressing any changes in substances used or work processes.

By understanding the nature of hazardous substances, complying with COSHH regulations, and implementing robust risk management strategies, contractors can create a workplace environment that prioritises safety, protects the health of their workforce, and mitigates the potential incidents associated with working with hazardous materials.

# Other Specific Activities and Advanced Technology

Now that we have covered the main types of hazardous activities, let's have a look at some other factors that should be considered.

## Lone Working

Lone working refers to situations where an employee works by themselves without direct supervision or immediate assistance. The concerns with lone working include:

- accidents, which could otherwise have been prevented had there been another worker there
- the worker may have an accident and be unable to communicate with other workers in another location.

The longer they are left alone, particularly with a serious injury, the more likely it is that they will be in significant danger.

The risk of lone workers must be managed, as stated in the Management of Health and Safety at Work Regulations. There are certain types of high risk work that must have at least one other person - such as confined spaces (in a supervisery/safety role), or near exposed live electricity conductors.

Considerations for lone working:

*Risk assessment*

- Identification of hazards: Assess potential risks and hazards associated with the specific tasks performed by lone workers.
- Remote locations: Consider the location—working alone in remote areas may pose different risks than in a populated area.

- Emergency procedures: Establish clear and effective emergency procedures, including how a lone worker can call for help.
- Check-ins: Implement regular check-ins via phone calls or automated systems to monitor and ensure the well-being of the lone worker, and provide a means for them to signal if assistance is required. Implement protocols for what to do if a check-in is missed.

*Training*

- Self-risk assessment: Train workers to assess and mitigate risks on their own, as they won't have immediate supervision.
- Emergency response: Provide training on proper responses to emergencies and first aid.

## Working with Cranes and Heavy Machinery

A significant feature of large contracts, such as multi storey new builds, is the use of cranes and heavy machinery. There are various hazards associated with these operations, including:

*Crushing and striking hazards*

Heavy machinery, including cranes, can crush or strike workers if they are caught between moving parts or pinned against structures or other equipment.

*Falling hazards*

Workers may fall from heights when operating or working near cranes or heavy machinery, especially during assembly, disassembly, or maintenance tasks conducted at elevated positions.

*Collapse hazards*

Improper operation or overloading of cranes and heavy machinery can lead to structural failures or collapses, endangering nearby workers and causing severe injuries or fatalities.

*Struck-by hazards*

Workers are at risk of being struck by moving loads, swinging equipment, or flying debris ejected from machinery during operation.

*Electrical hazards*

Cranes and heavy machinery may come into contact with overhead power lines, posing electrocution hazards to operators and nearby workers.

*Tipping hazards*

Cranes and heavy machinery can tip over if not properly stabilised or if operated on unstable ground, leading to rollover accidents with the potential for catastrophic consequences.

*Pinch point hazards*

Workers can be caught in pinch points between moving parts of machinery, such as gears, tracks, or hydraulic components, resulting in severe crushing or amputation injuries.

*Visibility hazards*

Limited visibility from the operator's cab can lead to accidents involving workers or obstacles in the machinery's path, particularly during manoeuvres or reverse operations.

*Noise hazards*

Operating cranes and heavy machinery generates high levels of noise, potentially causing hearing damage to workers if adequate hearing protection is not worn.

*Environmental hazards*

Adverse weather conditions, such as high winds, rain, snow, or extreme temperatures, can affect the stability and operation of cranes and heavy machinery, increasing the risk of accidents.

**Oversail Licenses for use of Cranes**

An oversail license is a legal agreement that permits the jib (arm) of a crane to swing over neighbouring properties or public spaces during construction projects. This license is essential when cranes are used in urban areas where space is constrained and the crane's operational area may extend beyond the boundaries of the construction site. The freehold ownership of land includes the air space above that land, so a contractor must negotiate an oversail licence otherwise the oversailing jib would be classed as trespass. The licence is usually an agreement between the contractor and the landowner. If the jib is to oversail public highways, then the oversail licence would also need to be entered into with the highway authority.

**Risk Management**
*Experience and training*
- Certification: Ensure operators are certified to operate specific machinery, meeting regulatory requirements.
- Continuous training: Provide ongoing training to keep operators updated on safety standards and equipment changes.

*Inspections*
- Regular maintenance: Schedule regular inspections and maintenance to identify and address potential issues before they become hazards.
- Pre-Operation Checks: Operators should perform pre-operation checks to ensure equipment is in proper working order.

*Communication*
- Clear signals: Establish standardised signals between equipment operators and ground personnel.
- Two-way communication: Ensure constant and clear communication between operators and other workers.

*Safety zones*
- Defined areas: Clearly mark and communicate safety zones around operating machinery.

- Restricted access: Limit access to these zones to authorised personnel only.

*PPE*

- High-Visibility Clothing: Ensure workers wear high-visibility clothing to enhance visibility, especially in busy construction sites.
- Hard Hats: Mandate the use of hard hats to protect against falling objects.

*Other*

- Implementing proper rigging and signalling procedures.
- Ensuring adherence to load capacity limits and safe operating practices.
- Monitoring and addressing environmental factors that may affect safe operations.
- Developing and rehearsing emergency response procedures in the event of an accident or equipment malfunction.

## Asbestos

UKATA and asbestos were mentioned briefly earlier in the book, let's now look at it in more detail. Asbestos, once used for its versatility and heat-resistant properties, was widely used in the construction of buildings in the past. It was incorporated into various building materials due to its strength, durability, insulation properties, and resistance to fire, chemicals, and electricity. However, the use of asbestos began to decline significantly in the late 20th century due to growing awareness of its health risks and the implementation of regulations restricting its use. The UK imposed a ban on the use of asbestos in new construction projects in 1999.

As of the present day, the use of asbestos is strictly regulated in the UK. While asbestos is no longer used in new construction projects, it remains present in many older buildings constructed before its ban. Efforts to manage and remove existing asbestos-containing materials from buildings and infrastructure continue to be a priority to minimise the risk of exposure.

Prior to the ban, asbestos was used in a variety of ways, such as for insulation, fireproofing, roofing materials (often still seen on old buildings constructed of asbestos cement sheets), flooring and coatings for ceilings and walls.

## Types of Asbestos

There are six types of asbestos minerals, categorised into two groups, the main types are white, blue and brown described below:

Serpentine asbestos:

Chrysotile (White asbestos): The most common form of asbestos, comprising long, curly fibres. Chrysotile asbestos was primarily used in the manufacturing of asbestos cement products, textiles, and friction materials.

Amphibole asbestos:

Crocidolite (Blue asbestos): Known for its long, straight fibres, crocidolite asbestos was commonly used in products such as cement sheets, insulation, and spray-on coatings.

Amosite (Brown asbestos): Amosite asbestos fibres are shorter and straighter than chrysotile fibres, making them suitable for use in insulation, cement products, and pipe insulation.

## Health Risks of Asbestos Exposure

Exposure to asbestos fibres poses severe health risks, including:

- Asbestosis is a chronic lung disease caused by the inhalation of asbestos fibres. It leads to inflammation and scarring of lung tissue, resulting in breathing difficulties, coughing, and chest pain.
- Lung Cancer - Inhalation of asbestos fibres increases the risk of developing lung cancer. Symptoms include persistent cough, chest pain, and difficulty breathing.

- Mesothelioma is a rare and aggressive cancer that affects the lining of the lungs, abdomen, or heart. It is primarily caused by exposure to asbestos and has a poor prognosis.

**Notifiable and Non-Notifiable Asbestos**

ACMs, or Asbestos-Containing Materials, are categorised as either notifiable or non-notifiable based on their risk level and the associated regulatory requirements.

Notifiable asbestos refers to ACMs that pose a higher risk of exposure during removal or remediation activities. These materials are considered more hazardous due to factors such as their friability (ease of releasing fibres), location, or the extent of disturbance required for removal. Notifiable asbestos includes:

High-risk materials:
- Asbestos insulation (e.g., sprayed coatings, pipe insulation).
- Loose asbestos materials (e.g., insulation board, loose-fill insulation).
- Asbestos insulation on boilers, ducts, and other equipment.

Friable materials:
- Asbestos-containing materials that are easily crumbled, pulverised, or reduced to powder by hand pressure.
- Any materials containing brown (amosite) or blue (crocidolite) asbestos.

Extensive disturbance:
- ACMs located in areas where significant disturbance or demolition is required for removal.
- Large-scale asbestos removal projects involving extensive areas or quantities of ACMs.

Under the asbestos regulations, any work around notifiable asbestos must be notified to the HSE at least 14 days before the work begins.

Removal or remediation of notifiable asbestos must be carried out by licensed asbestos removal contractors who have undergone specialised training and hold the necessary permits and equipment to safely handle and dispose of asbestos.

When undertaking work in an area with notifiable asbestos, the duty holder (such as the building owner or employer) must submit a notification to the HSE, providing details of the project scope, location, timetable, and precautions to be taken to minimise asbestos exposure.

Notifiable asbestos projects typically require comprehensive air monitoring before, during, and after the removal process to ensure that asbestos fibre levels remain below regulatory limits and protect the health and safety of workers and occupants.

Non-notifiable asbestos refers to ACMs that are considered lower risk in terms of exposure during removal or remediation activities. These materials may be firmly bound within a matrix (such as asbestos cement) or located in areas where they are unlikely to be disturbed.

Non-notifiable asbestos includes:

Lower-risk materials:

- Asbestos cement products (e.g., corrugated sheets, roof tiles, pipes).
- Asbestos-containing flooring materials (e.g., vinyl tiles, linoleum).
- Asbestos-containing textured coatings (e.g., "Artex" ceiling finishes) if firmly bound and in good condition.

Firmly bound materials:

- ACMs that are firmly bound within a matrix (e.g., asbestos cement), making fibre release unlikely under normal conditions.
- Materials where asbestos fibres are encapsulated or encased in a non-friable matrix.

Limited disturbance:
- ACMs located in areas where minimal disturbance is required for removal or maintenance.
- Small-scale projects involving the removal or encapsulation of limited quantities of ACMs.

While non-notifiable asbestos is still subject to regulations under CAR 2012 (Control of Asbestos Regulations 2012), the removal or remediation of these materials does not require notification to the enforcing authority. However, work must still be conducted in accordance with strict safety procedures and best practices. Although non-notifiable asbestos may pose a lower risk, it should only be handled by trained personnel with the appropriate knowledge and equipment to prevent fibre release and ensure safe handling and disposal.

Prior to undertaking work in an area with non-notifiable asbestos, a thorough risk assessment should be conducted to identify potential hazards, determine appropriate control measures, and ensure compliance with relevant regulations and guidelines.

It is essential to adhere to safe work practices, including proper PPE, containment measures, and waste disposal procedures.

## Risk Management
*Identification*
- Building surveys: Conduct thorough surveys to identify the presence and location of asbestos within buildings.
- Asbestos register: Maintain an asbestos register, documenting the type, location, and condition of asbestos-containing materials.

*Risk assessment*
- Material condition: Assess the condition of asbestos-containing materials to determine if they pose a risk of releasing fibres.

- Exposure pathways: Identify potential exposure pathways and implement controls to minimize the risk of inhalation.

*Safe removal*
- Licensed professionals: Hire licensed asbestos removal professionals for safe and legal removal.
- Containment measures: Implement stringent containment measures during removal to prevent the spread of asbestos fibres.

*Legal compliance*
- Regulatory knowledge: Stay informed about and comply with regulations regarding asbestos management, removal, and disposal.
- Notification procedures: Follow proper notification procedures when asbestos removal is planned.

It should be noted that not all contractors will be experienced, qualified or licenced in asbestos removal, and should they come across it during the course of a contract (for example, during a shop fit out), it is common to leave the site or area immediately and engage with asbestos removal contractors to handle and safely remove the ACM.

## Planned vs Reactive Maintenance

Planned (preventative) maintenance and reactive maintenance are two approaches to managing the upkeep and repair of assets, such as equipment, machinery, or facilities. Here's an explanation of each, the differences between them, and why reactive maintenance may pose more liability concerns than preventative maintenance. Planned maintenance involves systematically scheduling maintenance activities at predetermined intervals to prevent equipment failure, minimise downtime, and prolong the lifespan of assets. Maintenance activities may include routine inspections, lubrication, calibration, cleaning, and replacement of components or parts before they fail.

Reactive maintenance, also known as corrective maintenance or breakdown maintenance, involves responding to equipment failures or malfunctions as they occur, with repairs initiated only after a problem arises.

Reactive maintenance is characterised by an ad-hoc, "firefighting" approach, where repairs are conducted urgently to restore functionality and minimise disruption to operations.

Whilst every precaution can be taken to ensure the maintenance and upkeep of equipment and building features such as boiler and plumbing systems, accidents and breakdowns do happen. This is why a significant number of companies provide reactive maintenance, advertising that they are available 24/7 for emergencies.

Construction workers engaged in reactive maintenance face heightened risks compared to those involved in preventative maintenance activities. These risks stem from the nature of reactive maintenance, including the urgency to address equipment failures or malfunctions as they occur. Here's an explanation of the increased risks for contract workers during reactive maintenance:

*Unfamiliarity with work environment*

Construction workers may be deployed to various sites to address equipment breakdowns, often encountering unfamiliar environments, layouts, and operating procedures. Lack of familiarity with the work environment increases the risk of accidents, injuries, or incidents due to unfamiliar hazards or inadequate knowledge of emergency procedures.

*Limited preparation time*

Reactive maintenance tasks are often initiated urgently, leaving contractors with limited time for preparation, planning, or conducting thorough risk assessments. Rushed preparations may result in inadequate hazard identification, control measures, or PPE selection, increasing the likelihood of accidents or exposures to workplace hazards. Risk assessments may be cursory or incomplete, overlooking potential hazards or failing to consider all relevant factors. Inadequate risk assessments increase the likelihood of unforeseen dangers, uncontrolled hazards, or unsafe working conditions that pose risks to contractors health and safety.

*High-pressure situations*

The urgency to restore functionality and minimise downtime during reactive maintenance creates high-pressure situations for construction workers, leading to stress, fatigue, or distractions that may compromise safety. High-pressure environments may result in rushed decision-making, shortcutting procedures, or overlooking safety protocols to expedite repairs, increasing the risk of errors or accidents.

*Limited familiarisation with equipment*

Contractors engaged in reactive maintenance may encounter a wide range of equipment types, models, or configurations during service calls. Limited familiarity with specific equipment or systems may impede contractors' ability to diagnose problems accurately, perform repairs safely, or operate machinery effectively, increasing the risk of errors, malfunctions, or accidents.

*Lack of coordination and communication*

Reactive maintenance activities may involve multiple stakeholders, including contract workers, site personnel, supervisors, and client representatives. Inadequate coordination, communication breakdowns, or unclear instructions may lead to misunderstandings, conflicting priorities, or unsafe work practices, heightening the risk of accidents, incidents, or operational disruptions.

To mitigate the increased risks associated with reactive maintenance for contractors, organisations should prioritise safety, provide comprehensive training and orientation for construction personnel, conduct thorough risk assessments, establish clear communication channels, and ensure compliance with safety regulations and industry best practices. By fostering a safety-conscious culture and prioritising hazard identification and control, organisations can protect the health and well-being of contract workers and enhance overall workplace safety during reactive maintenance activities.

## Drones

The use of drones, also known as unmanned aerial vehicles (UAVs), in the construction industry has expanded significantly in recent years, offering various benefits and applications throughout the project lifecycle. Here are some of the ways that drones are used in construction:

*Aerial surveys and mapping*

Site planning and design:

Drones equipped with high-resolution cameras and LiDAR (Light Detection and Ranging) sensors can capture detailed aerial imagery and topographic data, facilitating site planning, design, and analysis.

Surveying and mapping:

Drones are used to conduct aerial surveys and create detailed topographic maps, orthomosaics (a map where a number of photos are overlapped to create a continuous image with distortions removed), and 3D models of construction sites, providing accurate spatial data for project planning, earthwork calculations, and infrastructure development.

Volume calculations:

Drone-based surveys enable accurate volume calculations which helps project managers optimise material quantities, reduce waste, and improve cost efficiency.

*Construction progress monitoring*

Progress tracking:

Drones capture aerial imagery and videos of construction sites at regular intervals, to monitor progress, track site conditions, and compare as-built conditions to design plans.

Workforce management:

Drones provide real-time visibility into on-site activities, to monitor workforce productivity, equipment utilisation, and adherence to safety protocols.

Quality assurance:

Aerial inspections conducted by drones help identify construction defects, deviations from specifications, and quality issues early in the construction process, allowing for timely corrective action and improved project outcomes.

*Safety and risk management*

Site safety inspections:

Drones conduct aerial inspections of construction sites, structures, and hard-to-reach areas, reducing the need for personnel to work at height or in hazardous environments, thereby improving worker safety and reducing the risk of accidents.

Emergency response:

Drones equipped with thermal imaging cameras and gas sensors assist in emergency response situations, such as search and rescue operations, fire monitoring, and disaster assessment, providing real-time situational awareness and enhancing safety.

*Asset management and maintenance*

Asset inspections:

Drones perform routine inspections of infrastructure assets, such as bridges, towers, and roofs, detecting defects, deterioration, and structural damage, allowing for proactive maintenance and extending asset lifespan.

**Considerations for the use of drones**

As technology continues to advance, drones are expected to play an increasingly integral role in shaping the future of construction practices and project delivery methodologies. The following considerations must be taken into account:

*Regulatory compliance*

Necessary permits and approvals must be obtained for drone usage as per regulations. There must also be an awareness and compliance with any flight restrictions in the area.

*Training*

Specific technical training for drone operation must be provided and recorded. Training must include safety protocols, emergency procedures, and the limitations of the technology.

*Privacy*

Drone operators must be aware of and comply with privacy laws when using drones.

*Communication*

Operators must ensure that they communicate the use of drones to individuals in the vicinity, especially if they might be recorded.

*Specific risk assessment*

Environmental factors must be considered, including weather conditions, airspace, and any obstacles that could impact safe drone operation. The battery life of the drone must be assessed and planned for to prevent unexpected shutdowns and potential damage or injury to third parties.

## Building Information Modelling (BIM)

Building Information Modelling is a digital representation of the physical and functional characteristics of a construction project. It's a collaborative process that utilises technology to generate and manage digital representations of the physical and functional characteristics of places.

BIM involves creating 3D digital models that encompass all aspects of a construction project, including the building's geometry, spatial relationships, materials, and components.

These models contain data and information about every element in the building, such as specifications, and maintenance requirements and architectural, structural, mechanical, electrical, and plumbing data.

BIM fosters collaboration among architects, engineers, contractors, and other project stakeholders by providing a shared platform for information exchange and decision-making.

This data integration can also assist in drawing up repair specifications if damage occurs.

BIM Level 2 signifies a crucial milestone in the adoption and implementation of Building Information Modelling (BIM) within the construction industry. It represents an advancement over BIM Level 1 in several key aspects:

*Interoperability and integration:* BIM Level 2 mandates the use of a Common Data Environment (CDE), providing a centralised platform for storing, managing, and sharing project information, and ensuring better control, access, and auditability of data.

*Collaboration and coordination:* BIM Level 2 encourages multi-disciplinary collaboration by enabling architects, engineers, contractors, and other stakeholders to work together on a federated BIM model. It also facilitates information sharing and transparency among project stakeholders through standardised processes and protocols. This promotes better decision-making, risk management, and value optimisation throughout the project lifecycle.

BIM Level 2 provides stakeholders with richer, more accurate information for decision-making and risk management.

BIM Level 2 compliance is mandated by government agencies or clients for publicly funded projects. These mandates aim to drive efficiency, productivity, and innovation within the construction industry by promoting the adoption of BIM technologies and processes.

The idea behind BIM was to assist in error reduction, however a lack of expertise and knowledge of the systems in all parts of the contract have prevented this from becoming a reality at this point in time.

## Smart Tools and Workwear

I read an interesting comment from an insurance article recently that stated that if a construction worker from 50 years ago were to be placed on a modern day construction site, they would not be lost or confused in the processes and activities undertaken. Where other industries have significantly increased their use of technology and innovation to improve productivity and efficiency, the construction industry has lagged behind in comparison.

They have, however, been increasingly adopting smart tools and workwear to enhance safety, efficiency, and productivity on site. These innovations incorporate advanced technologies to monitor environmental conditions, worker health, and equipment status.

### *Smart tools*

Vibration monitoring equipment: Monitors vibration levels to prevent hand-arm vibration syndrome (HAVS) in workers operating plant machinery. Sensors on plant or worn by operators (often as smart watches) can track and record vibration exposure. This helps in compliance with safety regulations, reduces the risk of HAVS, and ensures timely maintenance of equipment.

Environmental Condition Monitoring: Tracks environmental factors like temperature, humidity, dust levels, and noise on construction sites. There are portable and stationary sensors connected to a central monitoring system.

These ensure a safe working environment, helps in adhering to health and safety standards, and can trigger alerts when conditions exceed safe limits.

Tool Maintenance and Inspection Alerts: These keep track of when tools need maintenance, inspection, or battery recharge. There are tags and sensors that communicate with a central system. This will help prevent equipment failure, ensures compliance with statutory inspections, and optimises tool performance and lifespan.

### *Smart workwear*

Vital signs monitoring: Monitors workers' vital signs such as heart rate, body temperature, and respiratory rate. Again, these can be smart watches, but can also be wearable sensors integrated into PPE (e.g., vests, helmets). These provide real-time health data, early detection of potential health issues, and can trigger alerts for immediate medical attention.

Fall detection and reporting: Detects when a worker has fallen and automatically reports the incident. The main technology for this is an accelerometer embedded in helmets or harnesses, and may include additional sensors which can provide further fall data. This technology enables quick response to accidents, reduces the severity of injuries, and improves overall site safety.

Location tracking: Monitors the location of workers on a construction site. GPS and RFID systems (Radio Frequency Identification) are integrated into PPE. This helps to ensure workers are in safe zones, and improves emergency response times if they have been trapped or fallen in an area where they may not easily be found otherwise.

Centralised monitoring systems: These collect and analyse data from various smart tools and PPE. The technology used is the IoT (Internet of Things) platforms and cloud-based software. This provides a comprehensive overview of site conditions, worker health, and equipment status, enabling proactive decision-making and improved safety management.

Predictive maintenance: Uses data, stored within the tools battery, to predict when equipment will need maintenance. This reduces downtime, extends equipment life, and lowers maintenance costs.

***Examples of smart tools and workwear***

Smart helmets: Equipped with sensors for fall detection, location tracking, and environmental monitoring.

Wearable health monitors: Integrated into vests or wristbands to track vital signs and alert for health anomalies.

Connected power tools: Tools with built-in sensors that monitor usage, performance, and maintenance schedules.

Environmental sensors: Devices placed around the site to continuously monitor air quality, temperature, and noise levels.

There are numerous potential future trends that may have a significant impact, trends such as digitisation and automation, solutions to reduce reliance on skilled labour, and further improvements to Health and Safety. Underwriters and other insurance professionals should keep up to date with these innovations from the substantial amount of knowledge that can be obtained on insurance and construction websites.

# General Building Contractors

## Alteration, Repair and Renovation Contractors

Alteration and repair work involves modifications or improvements to existing structures. This can include renovations, extensions, or repairs to address structural issues. The skills involved will include a mixture of various trades such as carpentry, masonry, plumbing, or electrical work. The hazards involved with this will vary both with the activities being undertaken, and the location that they are being carried out. General hazards can include issues with structural integrity, use of tools, and presence of asbestos or other hazardous materials in older structures. In terms of training and qualifications, this will be skill specific, and some activities will not have associated qualifications, but rely heavily on training and experience. This will include an understanding of building regulations (and regular refresher training to ensure that contractors are aware of any updates to the regulations) and safety training for both themselves and the general public.

Their Health & Safety policy should include both generic and activity/location specific risk assessments, carrying out structural assessments, adherence to safety codes, ensuring stability during alterations, as well as safe handling and disposal of hazardous materials.

Building contractors engaged in alterations and repairs often face higher inherent risks compared to those involved in new builds. The existing core structure of a building introduces complexities and potential challenges that require careful consideration and skilled management.

**Factors Contributing to Higher Risk in Alterations/Repairs**

Alterations involve cutting into or modifying existing structures. Poorly executed alterations can compromise the structural integrity of the building and increase the potential for damage. Key aspects to consider include:

*Existence of core structure:*

- Alterations and repairs involve working with the existing framework of a building. Determining the structural integrity of an older or damaged structure requires a thorough assessment to identify potential weaknesses.
- The presence of pre-existing conditions, such as hidden structural deficiencies or outdated construction methods, can lead to unforeseen challenges during the alteration process.

*Unknown history and materials:*

- Older buildings, especially those lacking detailed documentation, may pose challenges in understanding the original construction methods, materials used, and any modifications made over time.
- The wear and tear on existing materials may result in hidden deterioration that becomes apparent only during the alteration process.

*Integration with existing systems:*

- Integrating new elements with the existing structure, such as updated electrical or plumbing systems, can be more complex than installing these systems in a new build and can create compatibility challenges.
- Unanticipated conflicts between new and existing systems may arise, requiring adjustments to ensure seamless integration.

- Repairs, especially those addressing specific issues, may require intrusive actions that could affect adjacent areas of the building.

**Risk Management Strategies**

*Comprehensive Assessments:*
- Pre-Construction Surveys - Conducting detailed surveys before starting alterations to identify potential structural issues and assess the overall condition of the building.
- Historical research - Gathering historical data on the building's construction and any modifications made over time to anticipate potential challenges.

*Skilled workforce:*
- Experienced contractors - Employing contractors with expertise in alterations and repairs, particularly those experienced in working with older or historical structures.
- Specialised trades - Engaging skilled tradespeople, such as masons or carpenters, familiar with traditional construction methods.

*Adherence to codes and standards:*
- Code compliance - Ensuring that all alterations and repairs comply with relevant building codes and standards.
- Quality assurance - Implementing rigorous quality assurance processes to verify that the alterations maintain or enhance the building's structural integrity.

**Alterations and Repairs to Historical or Listed Buildings**

The types of buildings that contractors work on can vary widely, ranging from residential homes to commercial or industrial properties. The complexity and potential hazards associated with these projects can depend on the specific characteristics of the buildings involved. In particular, preservation and restoration work on historical or listed buildings requires specialised knowledge.

### *What are listed buildings?*

A listed building is a structure recognised for its historical, architectural, or cultural significance. Listing is a way of legally protecting buildings and structures, ensuring their preservation for future generations. Buildings are classified into three grades in England, Wales, and Northern Ireland, while Scotland employs a slightly different system. Here's an overview of the grading system for listed buildings in each country.

*England, Wales, and Northern Ireland:*

Grade I:

Significance: Buildings of exceptional interest, only 2.5% of all listed buildings are Grade I.

Examples: Historic landmarks such as Westminster Abbey, Tower of London.

Grade II* (Grade Two Star):

Significance: Particularly important buildings, constituting about 5.5% of all listed buildings.

Examples: High-quality buildings like Albert Hall and St. Pancras Station.

Grade II:

Significance: Buildings of national importance and accounting for the majority of listed buildings (92%).

Examples: Many residential and commercial structures fall into this category.

*Scotland:*

Category A:

Significance: Buildings of national or international importance, making up around 8% of listed structures.

Examples: Edinburgh Castle, Glasgow School of Art.

Category B:

Significance: Buildings of regional or more than local importance, about 51% of listed structures.

Examples: Various residential and commercial properties.

Category C:

Significance: Buildings of local importance, constituting around 41% of listed structures.

Examples: Smaller, locally significant structures.

A Listed status aims to protect the architectural and historical features of a building. Alterations or demolition usually require special consent.

### *What are the specific concerns and risk management?*

Contractors may engage in carefully preserving architectural features, using authentic materials, and adhering to strict conservation guidelines. Specific considerations and risk management is required for work on these buildings, and contractors undertaking this work that do not have this specialist previous experience are unattractive to insurers. Factors that need to be considered include:

- Complex regulations: Working on listed or heritage buildings often involves navigating intricate regulations to preserve historical significance, and can involve lengthy delays whilst obtaining planning permission.
- Fragile materials: The use of delicate or outdated construction materials may increase the risk of damage during alterations or repairs.
- Difficulty in obtaining materials: When the exact construction material cannot be obtained, cheaper, more modern alternatives must be sought, but they must have the same aesthetic appearance as the original building.

- Preservation challenges: Preservation projects may demand specialised skills to maintain the building's authenticity while addressing structural issues.

*Risk management*
- Thorough assessment - Conducting a detailed assessment of the building's condition before commencing work.
- Specialised training - Ensuring that contractors possess the expertise required for heritage preservation.
- Collaboration - Working closely with preservation authorities to meet regulatory requirements.

## Other Key Locations to Consider

There are other types of locations that also need careful consideration due to some inherent features, some of the most common ones include the following types:

*Schools and healthcare facilities*

Educational institutions: Schools and universities may require alterations to accommodate changes in space utilisation or repairs to aging infrastructure. Contractors may need to work around academic schedules to minimise disruptions.

Healthcare facilities: Hospitals and clinics may need alterations to meet evolving healthcare needs or repairs to ensure compliance with safety standards. Sensitivity to patient care and infection control is paramount. These buildings often operate continuously, requiring contractors to execute alterations or repairs with minimal disruption to daily activities. Adhering to strict regulations in healthcare settings is crucial to maintaining patient safety and preventing disruptions to critical services.

*Risk management*

Phased approaches: Implementing phased construction to minimise disruptions.

Collaboration with stakeholders: Engaging with building occupants, staff, and administrators to co-ordinate projects effectively.

Adherence to standards: Ensuring strict adherence to healthcare regulations and guidelines for patient safety, or the building regulations set out for school buildings and grounds.

*Commercial and industrial spaces*

Structural complexity: Larger commercial or industrial buildings may have complex structures, requiring careful planning for alterations or repairs.

Occupational hazards: Industrial settings may pose additional hazards, such as working around heavy machinery, often operational as a production line, or dealing with specialised materials.

*Risk management*

Detailed planning: Developing comprehensive plans to address structural complexities. Thorough RAMS developed to ensure no or minimal disruption to production.

Safety protocols: Implementing robust safety protocols to mitigate risks associated with machinery or hazardous materials.

## New Build Contractors

New builds involve the construction of entirely new structures, whether residential, commercial, or industrial. This includes the entire process from initial design to completion. From the outset, the skillset needs to include project management, structural engineering, and architectural design. The equipment used can vary greatly, from heavy plant such as excavators or tower cranes, to power hand tools. Building materials can vary greatly, and formwork may be used as a temporary structure for concrete buildings.

The hazards can vary greatly depending on these features, as well as activities such as working at height, and exposure to construction materials that can pose respiratory risks.

The training or qualifications involved may be a construction-related degree or apprenticeship, or activity specific training. There will also be a requirement to understand the building codes and regulations, and safety training for construction environments.

Risk management features will include structural integrity considerations, proper use of PPE, and regular safety briefings and site inspections.

# A-Z of Ancillary Trades

Let us now explore some specific trades, what they involve, their inherent risks, and typical risk management features.

## Air Conditioning, Heating, and Ventilation Contractors

These contractors specialise in the installation, maintenance, and repair of HVAC (Heating, Ventilation, and Air Conditioning) systems in buildings, ensuring optimal indoor climate control. The skills involved include HVAC system design and installation, knowledge of refrigerants and heating elements, diagnostic and troubleshooting skills. The equipment used will include HVAC units, ductwork, thermostats, refrigerant recovery equipment, testing and measurement tools.

There are several hazards to consider for this type of trade. They are likely to undertake heat work, and often will work at heights for duct installation. There is also the potential for refrigerant exposure and incidents relating to electrical systems. Working at industrial locations will add additional hazards.

Training and qualifications for this type of trade can include HVAC certification, understanding of electrical systems, and safety training in handling refrigerants, in addition to training for height and heat work.

Risk management procedures will include adherence to safety regulations and their site specific RAMS.

Oftec is a registration body for technicians working in the heating and renewable energy industries. Oftec registration signifies competence in the installation and maintenance of oil-fired and renewable heating systems.

## Bricklayers

Bricklayers are skilled tradespeople who lay bricks, concrete blocks, and other masonry materials to construct walls, buildings, or other structures. They are skilled in bricklaying techniques, mortar mixing and application, and interpretation of architectural plans. The equipment used will include trowels, hammers and levels, mortar mixers, scaffolding and masonry saws.

This is sometimes considered a lower hazard trade, however they are still susceptible to physical strain and repetitive motion injuries, exposure to dust and debris during cutting and mixing, falls from working at heights on scaffolding.

Training can involve an apprenticeship or vocational training, construction safety, interpreting blueprints.

Risk management will cover generic and site specific hazards, including regular equipment maintenance.

## Cabling Contractors

Cabling contractors specialise in the installation and maintenance of various types of cables, including data cables, electrical wiring, and telecommunication cables. The skills involved include cable installation and termination, understanding of electrical systems, network cabling and infrastructure.

Their equipment may comprise cabling materials (copper, fiber-optic), cable termination tools, or testing equipment (multimeters, cable testers). The main hazards involved will be work at depth, electrical hazards, potential exposure to data or communication lines, and working in confined spaces.

They will have a knowledge of electrical systems, a cabling and wiring certification, and safety training for working with cables. Their risk management will include checking for the locations of cables and services, and ensuring safety when working near electrical systems. If they undertake work in server rooms then site

169

specific RAMS are paramount to avoid damage and potential large losses.

## Carpenters and Joiners (including Studwork)

Carpenters and joiners work with wood to construct and install structures, furniture, and fittings.

They use woodworking and joinery techniques, and have knowledge in reading and interpreting blueprints, precision cutting and shaping of wood. Their equipment tends to incorporate hand tools (saws, chisels), Power tools (drills, routers), and woodworking machinery (lathes, planers).

The main hazards can include power tool injuries, dust exposure during cutting and sanding, and manual handling injuries.

Training normally involves a carpentry or joinery apprenticeship, and they must also gain a knowledge of building codes and regulations, as well as safety training for tool operation.

Risk management will include proper use of PPE and regular equipment inspections and maintenance.

Studwork is an activity that can be undertaken by a variety of different contractors, as it is not generally a standalone trade. For simplicity I have linked it to carpenters, however it can be undertaken by partitioning contractors, internal fitters, or general building contractors.

Also known as stud framing or stud wall construction, this is a common method used to create interior partition walls, room dividers, or structural frames. It involves assembling a framework of vertical and horizontal members, known as studs and plates respectively, to form the basic structure of a wall. Studs are typically made of wood or metal (such as timber or steel), and are the primary load-bearing components of studwork walls. They are positioned at regular intervals along the length of the wall, spaced apart to accommodate doorways, windows, or other openings.

Hazards include manual handling injuries from lifting heavy materials, cuts and lacerations from sharp tools, falls from heights while installing studs or plates, and exposure to dust and fumes from cutting or sanding materials.

Risk management will include appropriate PPE, manual handling training including use of mechanical aids, fall protection, tool safety and dust control.

## Cavity Wall Insulators

Cavity wall insulators, soundproofing experts, and insulation contractors contribute to creating more energy-efficient, comfortable, and acoustically sound living and working spaces. Cavity wall insulation involves the installation of insulating materials within the cavity (gap) between the inner and outer walls of a building. The goal is to improve thermal efficiency, reducing heat loss and energy consumption. Insulation materials, such as foam or mineral wool, are injected or placed into the wall cavities. Small holes are drilled into the mortar, and then injected with the insulation material into the cavity. If there are any damp problems, this must be resolved before the walls are insulated.

Contractors must have good installation techniques and knowledge of insulation materials.

The inherent hazards for this type of work include:
- Chemical exposure from insulation materials.
- Confined spaces when working within wall cavities.
- Respiratory hazards where they may encounter dust and airborne particles during the installation process.
- Fall hazards where they undertake installations in elevated areas.

Training may include a vocational qualification such as NVQ Level 2 qualification in Insulation and Building Treatments, as well as Confined Space Entry Training.

Risk management will include the following in addition to general H&S measures:

Site assessment: Thoroughly assessing the worksite for potential risks before installation.

Proper ventilation: Ensuring adequate airflow during insulation work.

Use of PPE: Including respiratory protection and fall protection.

Material Safety Data Sheets (MSDS): Providing information on the safe use of insulation materials.

## Civil Engineers

Civil engineering involves the design, construction, and maintenance of infrastructure projects that serve the public. This can include projects like roads, bridges, dams, buildings, and water supply systems. Civil engineers apply scientific and mathematical principles to develop and implement plans that enhance and sustain communities. Their skills include engineering design, project management and surveying.

The equipment used can consist of surveying instruments, heavy machinery (excavators, bulldozers), and construction materials. This trade is considered a heavier one, particularly where significant infrastructure is being built or worked upon, such as bridges or dams, as these have the potential for significant losses from injuries or damage.

Other specific hazards include excavation and trenching work, heavy equipment operation,
working in adverse weather and challenging terrains.

Qualifications can include a civil engineering degree, common for engineers overseeing projects, in addition to the general qualifications mentioned earlier.

Additional risk management may include identifying and mitigating potential environmental risks, and comprehensive emergency response planning, preparing for unforeseen events such as adverse weather conditions.

## Cladding Contractors

Cladding contractors specialise in the installation of exterior cladding systems, which provide protective and aesthetic coverings for buildings. This can include materials such as metal, composite panels, or other cladding solutions. The skills required include an understanding of architectural plans, weatherproofing and sealing techniques. The equipment used will include the cladding materials, fastening tools (screws, rivets), and access equipment (scaffolding, lifts).

The main hazards will include working at heights, use of power tools and potential exposure to weather elements. There is a specific NVQ course for CSCS Roofing and Cladding which addresses safety training for work at height.

Since the tragedy of Grenfell Tower, there has been a spotlight on the quality and safety of cladding materials. In 2018 the government announced the ban of combustible materials for use in cladding of high rise buildings, and the Building Safety Act was released in 2022 which changed legislation in relation to high risk buildings. It is the most comprehensive legislation to be introduced to the building industry in decades. It requires a higher level of competency in contractors, particularly principal designers and contractors, building control professionals, quantity surveyors and project managers. Whilst it only applies in England, the rest of the UK have also taken preventative steps to ensure safer buildings.

## Cleaning Contractors

Cleaning contractors provide ongoing cleaning services for buildings, which can be internal or external. Cleaning agents can range from non-hazardous such as water, to industrial cleaning materials.

External cleaning of buildings can involve the use of water, chemicals, or compressed air. It may involve cleaning of listed or heritage buildings which carries the potential for higher claims costs.

Internal cleaners can cover a range of premises, such as residential, hotels, offices, shops, more complex locations like industrial or manufacturing premises, or more specialist locations like hospitals. This could involve the removal of hazardous waste or sharps. This trade can vary greatly in terms of how hazardous it is depending on method and materials used, locations worked, and the activities involved, so it is important to fully understand a companies specific work exposures.

The main hazards for contractors are exposure to cleaning agents and manual handling, sometimes also working at height. For both contractors and third parties, there is also the potential for slips, trips, and falls. Third party damage could occur from improper use of cleaning materials, or from high pressure spraying.

Risk management should include COSHH assessments, and appropriate risk assessments to mitigate the risk of slips, trips and falls. This will normally involve cordoned off areas and/or clearly visible signage for the area to avoid.

### Curtain Walling Contractors

Curtain walling is a non-structural outer covering of a building's façade, typically made of lightweight materials like glass, aluminium, or steel. It is designed to provide an aesthetically pleasing appearance while allowing natural light into the building. Contractors must have a working knowledge of installation of framing systems and glazing, as well as being fully trained and qualified in working at height and manual handling.

The equipment used can include aluminium or steel frames, glass panels, sealants, framing tools and glass handling equipment. Hazards include a risk of falls from height as often contractors are working at elevated levels.

Handling large glass panels or other materials can lead to musculoskeletal injuries, there is also the potential hazard of accidental damage to the glass panels.

The use of power tools and heavy equipment introduces the risk of cuts, crush injuries, and other accidents.

Risk management can include:

Fall protection systems: Installing guardrails, safety nets, or personal fall arrest systems.

Regular equipment inspections: Ensuring that tools and equipment are well-maintained and safe to use, adhering to installation standards and maintain structural integrity.

Site-specific risk assessments: Identifying and addressing hazards unique to each project, ensuring sealing for weather resistance, and documentation of glass movement and handling procedures to ensure reduction in likelihood of broken glass panels.

## Damp Proofing Installers

Damp proofing installers focus on preventing and remedying issues related to dampness and moisture in buildings. This includes the installation of damp-proofing courses and membranes.

They need to be able to identify damp issues, have a working knowledge of building structures and have experience in installing damp-proofing materials.

The hazards for this trade include exposure to damp and mould, working at heights, and use of tools for structural alterations.

Contractors should have damp proofing certification or training and safety training should include working at heights. Their risk management will involve proper use of PPE including respiratory equipment to prevent inhalation of dangerous substances - there is potential for exposure to asbestos. They must therefore have a stringent safety policy and strict method procedures to ensure adherence to safety guidelines and regulations.

## Drains, Sewers, Water Treatment, etc. - Refurbishment, New Construction

This trade involves the construction, refurbishment, and maintenance of drains, sewers, and water treatment facilities for the effective management of wastewater and stormwater. Contractors must have experience and training in the installation and maintenance of drainage systems, knowledge of sewer systems, and water treatment techniques. Their equipment will include that for excavation and trenching, pipe materials (concrete, PVC), and water treatment systems.

The hazards that face are exposure to wastewater, working at depth or in confined spaces,
and potential exposure to hazardous substances. These contractors will require drainage or civil engineering training or qualifications and safety training for these particular types of environments. Their risk management must include proper safety measures for trenching and excavation, use of specific PPE, and compliance with environmental regulations.

## Drain/Tank Cleaning Contractors

Drain and tank cleaning contractors specialise in cleaning and maintaining drainage systems, tanks, and other storage facilities to ensure proper function and prevent blockages or contamination. Their skills include operation of cleaning equipment, knowledge of drainage systems, and hazardous waste management. They use high-pressure water jets, and vacuum and suction equipment.

The hazards they face are in common with the previous trade, exposure to hazardous materials and working in confined spaces as well as potential exposure to harmful gases.

Contractors must have training in drain and tank cleaning and hazardous waste management certification. They must also have confined space entry training where relevant.

Their risk management must include use of specific PPE, COSHH assessments and proper disposal of waste materials.

## Electrical Contractors

Electricians install and maintain electrical systems, generally in buildings. This is a trade that can vary greatly, from a general electrical contractor working on domestic properties only, to a specialist in 3 phase work at industrial locations, to a specialist installing security equipment.

They must all have skills in and working knowledge of wiring, circuit design, and knowledge of electrical codes. The equipment will include wire and wiring tools, multimetres, and electrical panels.

The general hazards include electrical fires, electric shocks, incorrect installation or rewiring causing faults in the system.

Training and qualifications will often start with an electrical apprenticeship or training course,
understanding of electrical codes and regulations, and safety training for electrical work.

Their risk management will include adherence to electrical safety protocols, use of PPE, regular inspections of electrical systems, and specific precautions for three-phase systems.

### 3 Phase Electrical Work

This work involves handling three-phase power systems commonly used in industrial settings. 3 phase systems have higher voltages compared to single-phase systems, increasing the severity of potential hazards. Contractors use insulated tools designed for use in high-voltage environments, 3-phase and voltage testers, non-contact voltage detectors.

The main hazards include arc flash incidents*, electrical shocks, and imbalances in the system leading to overheating and equipment failure.

There isn't a specific standalone qualification exclusively for 3-phase electrical work. Instead, 3-phase electrical work typically falls under the broader umbrella of electrical qualifications and certifications. Individuals working with 3-phase electrical systems usually obtain qualifications that cover general electrical principles and practices, and they gain additional experience or training specific to 3-phase installations.

Their risk management must include use of specific PPE - insulated gloves and arc flash clothing.

* An arc flash incident is a sudden release of intense energy caused by an electric arc. This phenomenon occurs when an electric current flows through the air between conductors or from a conductor to a ground. The released energy produces a flash of light and heat, along with a powerful blast of pressure and sound. Arc flash incidents are associated with high temperatures, intense light, and can result in serious injuries, burns, and damage to equipment.

### Alarm and CCTV Installation

Alarm installation is a specialised field involving the planning, installing, and maintaining of alarm systems for residential and commercial properties tailored to the unique needs of their clients. Alarm installers assess the property, collaborate with clients to determine security needs based on potential vulnerabilities, install sensors and components, conduct thorough testing, and provide ongoing maintenance to ensure optimal system performance. Integration with other security features, such as lighting controls or access control systems, is also part of the installation process. The process for CCTV installation includes a site survey, cooperation with clients to understand surveillance objectives, mounting cameras, configuring systems for optimal performance, conducting testing, and educating clients on system operation. Post-installation, CCTV installers may provide routine maintenance to keep the system in peak condition. This can include software updates, camera adjustments, and troubleshooting support. Their equipment will include cable tester wire tracers, and motion detector testers. The hazards they face may include an increased risk of errors from installing complex systems, improper installation could lead to false alarms, impacting system reliability and increasing potential risk of claims from third parties. They may also be involved in work at height and manual handling.

There is specialised training in alarm system/CCTV installation and the specific alarm systems/CCTV systems used. Risk management procedures include use of PPE, completing RAMS, security measures appropriate for the environment, regular training and review of risk management strategies.

### Efficacy

Efficacy is a critical consideration in the electrical contracting industry, as electrical work is associated with potential risks, safety concerns, and the need for compliance with electrical codes. Efficacy requires electrical contractors to comply with national regulations governing electrical installations. This includes obtaining necessary permits, approvals, and certifications for their work.

Keeping accurate records and documentation is part of demonstrating efficacy. Contractors should maintain records of installations, inspections, and tests, providing a comprehensive history of their work for future reference.

Whilst general electrical contractors have to consider fire risks, energy efficiency, voltage stability, and the proper functioning of electrical components, those installing security or fire systems carry a greater risk in terms of efficacy.

Where electrical contractors are undertaking fire or intruder alarm installations, CCTV, or sprinkler installations, efficacy refers to the requirement that the security and safety systems operate reliably, meet industry standards, and fulfil the intended purpose of protecting life and property.

Electrical contractors must demonstrate competence in:

- designing and installing systems that are tailored to the specific needs and risks of the property. This includes placing sensors, cameras, alarms, and sprinklers strategically to maximise coverage and effectiveness.
- the seamless integration of multiple systems. For example, integrating fire alarms with sprinklers or coordinating CCTV and intruder alarm systems to enhance overall security.
- Thorough testing and commissioning of the installed systems must take place to ensure that all components function as intended, and any issues are identified and addressed before the systems are declared operational.
- ensuring that the installed systems are reliable and durable. Components such as detectors, alarms, cameras, and sprinkler heads must be of high quality and capable of withstanding environmental conditions.

Other factors to consider include:

*Training and user education* - Contractors should provide training to end-users on how to operate and maintain the installed systems.

Contractors must ensure that users are well-informed about system functionalities, emergency procedures, and routine maintenance requirements.

*Emergency response* - The efficacy of security and safety systems is measured by their ability to trigger timely and appropriate responses in case of an incident. For example, fire alarms should activate sprinklers and alert emergency services promptly.

*Comprehensive risk assessment* - Before installation, contractors must conduct a comprehensive risk assessment of the property to identify potential security or safety threats. Efficacy involves tailoring the systems to address specific risks and vulnerabilities.

*Ongoing maintenance and monitoring* - Efficacy is an ongoing commitment that includes regular maintenance and monitoring of installed systems. Contractors should provide scheduled inspections, address any issues promptly, and ensure that systems remain in optimal working condition.

*Documentation and compliance records* - Contractors must maintain thorough documentation of installations, tests, and compliance records. This documentation is essential for demonstrating efficacy, ensuring traceability, and meeting regulatory requirements.

## Differences Between Work at Domestic, Commercial and Industrial Locations

Domestic hazards:
- Common electrical hazards such as shocks and fires.
- Limited scale but still a risk of injury or property damage.

Commercial:
- Increased scale compared to domestic settings.
- Use of complex electrical systems for lighting, HVAC, and equipment.
- Higher foot traffic, posing a risk of accidental damage.

Industrial:
- High-powered machinery and equipment pose severe electrical risks.
- Potential for arc flashes and explosions in certain industries.
- Complex electrical systems with a higher probability of faults.

All of these activities have risk management procedures in common - RAMS, training, PPE, etc. but they also have some specific measures that need to be carried out to address the specific challenges posed.

### Accreditations and Qualifications
NICEIC
The National Inspection Council for Electrical Installation Contracting, is a leading electrical certification body in the UK. NICEIC is renowned for assessing and certifying electrical contractors, electricians, and electrical installation work. The organisation plays a crucial role in ensuring the safety and quality of electrical installations in both domestic and commercial settings. The key aspects of NICEIC are:

*Assessment and certification*
NICEIC provides certification for electrical contractors and businesses engaged in electrical installation work. Sole trading electricians can also seek certification from NICEIC, demonstrating their competence in carrying out electrical installations.

*Regulatory compliance*
Adherence to regulations - NICEIC-certified contractors and electricians are expected to adhere to the latest electrical

regulations and standards, including the Wiring Regulations (BS 7671), as well as compliance with relevant building regulations.

*Safety and competence*

NICEIC ensures that its certified contractors maintain high safety standards in their electrical work. Contractors and electricians undergo assessments to demonstrate their technical competence and knowledge of industry best practices.

*Consumer confidence*

NICEIC certification is widely recognised brand and trusted by consumers, building owners, and regulatory authorities. Choosing an NICEIC-certified contractor provides assurance to clients that the electrical work will be carried out to the highest standards of safety and quality.

*Comprehensive range of services*

NICEIC certification covers a broad spectrum of work in various sectors, such as residential, commercial, industrial, and public sectors.

*Training and technical support*

NICEIC supports continuous professional development for electricians through training programs and certified members have access to a range of resources, including technical advice and updates on industry best practices.


The Fire and Security Association

The FSA comprises members from the Electrical Contractors Association (ECA) and its Scottish counterpart, SELECT. The ECA provides comprehensive support to its members, offering guidance on health and safety, regulatory standards, and an extensive list of other matters. Collaborating closely with regulatory bodies, the ECA strives to establish a secure and efficient industry.

Functioning as a specialised group within the ECA, the FSA operates in collaboration with SELECT (The Scottish Electrical Contractors Association), delivering national representation and unparalleled expertise for professionals involved in the design, installation, commissioning, maintenance, and monitoring of fire, emergency, and security systems.

FSA membership is open to companies that have attained the highest certification levels in the Fire, Security, or Monitoring centre fields - through 'approved' industry certification bodies. This pertains specifically to fire detection and alarm systems, as well as emergency and escape lighting.

Membership categories encompass:

Electronic security systems (including intruder, hold-up, and social alarms, CCTV, and access control systems), and

Emergency, fire detection, and alarm systems.

To qualify for FSA membership, companies need a minimum one-year trading history and a specified level of competence - full details can be found on the relevant website.

As for SELECT, the Scottish equivalent, all applicants undergo scrutiny by Technical Advisers who inspect their work to ensure compliance with standards. Additionally, a commercial audit is conducted to ascertain that firms seeking membership are well-managed and financially viable, with a minimum establishment period of six months.

*Importance of FSA membership*

Obtaining memberships in the FSA, along with relevant certifications, holds significant importance for electrical contractors involved in alarm, CCTV, and sprinkler installation. They demonstrate a commitment to high standards, professionalism, and continuous improvement in the field of fire and security systems. The significance can be outlined in the following ways:

Expertise and competence:

FSA memberships require contractors to meet specific competency standards. This assures clients and insurers that the contractors possess the necessary skills and expertise to design, install, and maintain alarm, CCTV, and sprinkler systems effectively.

Adherence to industry standards:

By being part of the FSA, contractors commit to adhering to industry standards and best practices. This can result in installations that meet or exceed regulatory requirements, reducing the risk of system failures or inefficiencies.

Quality Assurance:

Contractors with these credentials are more likely to deliver reliable and effective fire and security systems, which is crucial for insurers assessing the risk associated with providing coverage.

Risk mitigation:

Insurers are concerned with minimising risks associated with property damage and loss. Contractors who are members of reputable associations are more likely to follow stringent safety protocols, reducing the likelihood of system failures, false alarms, or inadequate protection.

Access to industry updates:

Membership provides contractors with access to the latest industry trends, technological advancements, and regulatory changes. This ongoing education ensures that contractors stay current with the evolving landscape of fire and security systems.

Streamlined approval processes:

Insurers may find it more straightforward to approve coverage for contractors who are members of recognised associations. This is because these contractors are perceived as having already undergone a vetting process, making them more reliable and trustworthy in the eyes of insurers.

Reduced liability:

For insurers, contractors with this membership indicates a lower risk of liability associated with system malfunctions or inadequate installations. This can positively impact insurance premiums and coverage terms.

## Exhibition Stand Erectors

Exhibition stand erection involves the assembly and installation of temporary structures for events, trade shows, or exhibitions. These contractors are skilled in precise assembly and installation, understanding of design plans, and ensuring public safety. The usual hazards include working at height, use of power tools, and manual handling of materials.

From a third party perspective, contractors must ensure that all equipment is secured properly, and stringent checks are carried out to ensure the safety of the public and third party property.

Locations worked at can vary from retail outlets, to large theatres and concert halls, to stadiums. It is important to understand the footfall of the locations worked at, as any claims costs can be compounded by the amount of people at the location at the time of the incident. For this reason, large audiences would be a detracting feature due to the possibility of multiple injuries from one incident. Rigging and lighting installation for concerts would be particularly unattractive to insurers due to the potential for third party injuries to music or theatre acts (where injury costs can be particularly high due to potential loss of earnings) and damage to expensive equipment on stage or in surrounding areas.

Training tends to involve carpentry or other construction training and safety training for event environments. Their risk management will include fall protection measures and ensuring of equipment safety.

# Fencing Contractors

Fencing contractors specialise in the design, installation, and maintenance of fencing and barriers for various purposes, including security, privacy, and aesthetic enhancement. They are skilled in fencing design and installation, have a working knowledge of different fencing materials, and carry out site assessments for fencing needs.

The equipment used will include fencing materials (wood, metal, vinyl), digging and post-setting equipment and hand tools for assembly.

The hazards for contractors can include working at depth (generally up to a metre for fencing post foundations), working with power tools, and manual handling of heavy materials.

With regards to the risk to the public, this can vary significantly depending on materials used, the locations and purposes of the fencing, as well as the amount of public access. Installation of automated barriers or gates can pose an additional risk to the public as faulty equipment could cause crush injuries, so it is important to understand the complexity of the contracts that are undertaken.

Contractors will have some form of fencing or general construction training, as well as safety training for outdoor environments.

Their risk management will include safe procedures for avoiding damage to underground cables, as well as compliance with safety regulations for working at depth.

# Flooring and Screeding Contractors

Flooring contractors specialise in the installation, repair, and maintenance of various types of flooring materials, including tiles, carpet, hardwood, laminate and cement. They are skilled in flooring installation techniques, surface preparation and levelling, and have a knowledge of different flooring materials. The equipment used includes cutting tools (saws, carpet knives), installation tools (trowels, adhesive applicators), floor sanders and polishers.

For screeding contractors, they will have cement mixers and screeding tools. Screeding may take place prior to the installation of other finishes such as tiles or carpets, or may be left as a basic concrete floor. Screeding contractors use various methods to apply screed, including traditional sand and cement screed, self-levelling screed, and polymer-modified screed. The method chosen depends on the requirements of the project and the desired finish.

Common materials used in screeding include cement, sand, water, and additives such as fibres or plasticisers to improve strength, workability, and drying times.

Hazards can include exposure to adhesives, chemicals and finishing materials, injuries from cutting and handling tools, respiratory issues from dust, and manual handling.

Training is usually from an apprenticeship or vocational training. The risk management procedures adopted should include proper ventilation or dust extraction during installation, safe handling of chemicals to avoid skin irritation or burns, and use of appropriate PPE. They will also need to ensure there is appropriate signage in the area to reduce the risk of third party incidents.

## Formwork and Shuttering Contractors

Formwork or shuttering contractors are involved in the construction of moulds or frameworks into which concrete is poured and shaped during the construction of structures like walls, columns, and slabs. The skills required are formwork design and construction, concrete pouring and finishing, and understanding of structural plans. These contractors use formwork materials (plywood, steel), reinforcement bars, and concrete mixing and pouring equipment.

One of the main hazards from this trade is chemical burns caused by handling of concrete, and the potential exposure to wet concrete which can cause respiratory issues. Often, they will also be working at heights.

Contractors will have formwork or carpentry training and safety training for working with concrete. Their risk management will include proper installation and bracing of formwork, and regular inspection of formwork integrity, and appropriate use of PPE is essential.

## Glazing Contractors including Conservatory Erection

Glazing contractors are involved in the construction and installation of windows, conservatories, and similar structures. They will be skilled in the construction and assembly of framing, glazing and sealing techniques, and knowledge of structural requirements.

Their equipment will include framework materials (metal, wood), glazing materials (glass, polycarbonate), and hand tools (saws, drills).

The hazards involved with this trade include injury from manual handling, working at heights, and potential exposure to glass or other materials. There is also an increased risk of accidental damage to the glass, so proper handling and securing is imperative. Contractors will have carpentry or other construction training. Their risk management will include fall protection measures, manual handling training, and ensuring compliance with building codes.

## Groundworkers

Groundworkers general activities include preparing construction sites for building work, or installing cables or services below ground. Activities include excavation, laying foundations, drainage installation, and groundwork for various structures. More specialist groundworking activities would generally fall under civil engineering.

The skills required include operation of excavation machinery, grading (the process of shaping and levelling the ground surface to meet the desired specifications for construction or landscaping), and knowledge of drainage systems. The equipment they use may include bulldozers, compaction equipment, and trenching tools. The main hazards are:

- Excavation - Risks of cave-ins, falls, or engulfment during trenching and excavation work.
- Hand-Arm Vibration Syndrome (HAVS) - Caused by prolonged use of vibrating tools.
- Utility strikes - Accidental damage to underground utilities during excavation.

The training and qualifications needed will include Construction Plant Competence Scheme (CPCS), confined space training, and first aid training.

Their risk management procedures will need to include:

- Use of protective systems such as shoring, sloping, or trench boxes to prevent collapses and maintain site stabilisation.
- Utility surveys to identify and mark the location of underground services before excavation.
- Regular health surveillance, to monitor workers for signs of HAVS and taking preventive measures.

## Landscape Gardeners and Tree Surgeons

Landscape gardeners design, plan, and implement outdoor spaces, including gardens, parks, and green areas. They are involved in planting, hardscaping, and maintaining outdoor environments. Tree surgeons are engaged in the maintenance of trees, and when necessary, their removal. The skills involved include landscape design, horticulture, knowledge of irrigation systems, tree surgery and tree felling techniques.

The main hazards for landscaping include manual handling, use of power tools (such as lawnmowers or chainsaws), and chemical exposure from handling fertilisers, pesticides, and other chemicals. For tree surgeons, the main concerns are working at heights (usually not from fixed platforms and therefore considered a high hazard activity), exposure to falling branches, and potential contact with hazardous plant materials. For tree felling, the hazards include falling debris and potential injury to third parties or property damage.

The training and qualifications include:

- Landscape Industry Certified Technician: Recognises expertise in various aspects of landscape work.
- Pesticide Application Certification: Required for those using or applying pesticides.
- Arboriculture courses: Specialised education in tree care, surgery, and felling techniques.

The risk management for these contractors should include proper lifting techniques, and chemical handling protocols. For tree surgeons, they should also ensure use of specialist PPE including fall arrest equipment, site specific RAMS to evaluate potential hazards, including the assessment of the direction of tree fall. They should also ensure they are equipped to handle emergency situations, such as unexpected tree falls or injuries.

## Mechanical Engineers

Mechanical engineers design, analyse, and oversee the implementation of mechanical systems. In construction, mechanical engineering in its purest sense is working on industrial plant and machinery, however it can also be used to describe work on HVAC systems or plumbing, so it is important to understand the activities undertaken by the contractor.

They can be installing, commissioning, monitoring, repairing and maintaining various industrial plant such as production machinery and systems. Work on production lines can be an enhanced risk from a public liability perspective as potential claims costs can be significant. It is also common for work to be undertaken at hazardous locations such as oil and gas industries, so it is imperative to ascertain where they carry out contracts. This is a complex trade, and with it carries a myriad of possible hazards, so the more information that can be obtained from contractors to understand their specific business, the easier it will be in considering the risks associated with that business.

Qualifications can include a mechanical engineering degree or other engineering degree. Mechanical engineers require technical expertise and most often, project management skills.

Risk management will include adherence to specific safety regulations at third party locations.

**Painters and Decorators**

Painters and decorators enhance the aesthetic appeal of surfaces through painting, wallpapering, and other decorative finishes. They are skilled in surface preparation and painting techniques. The hazards include chemical exposure, working at heights, and respiratory risks.

Additional consideration should be given if they paint externally, and the different hazards this can present to the public and third party property.

Training is generally by way of a painting and decorating apprenticeship or training. Their risk management must include proper ventilation, use of appropriate PPE, and avoidance of damage from spray drift.

## Plant Hire

Plant hire involves renting out heavy machinery and equipment for construction, excavation, and earthmoving purposes. Plant hire companies provide a range of machinery for short-term or long-term use. The skills required include equipment operation, maintenance, and logistics.

The equipment used can include a variety of heavy machinery such as excavators, bulldozers, cranes, loaders.

The hazards involved where the plant is hired out without a driver include those associated with moving and transporting large equipment and routine maintenance and repair activities.

Where drivers are provided along with the plant, the hazards are akin to those of a groundworker or other plant operator - injuries to contractors or the public caused by heavy machinery, damage to the machinery, etc.

Those hired out under CPA conditions would be preferential to insurers, due to the standardised nature of the contract that ensures that both the hiring company and the plant hire company meet industry best practices for safety and quality. It would ensure adequate equipment inspection and maintenance and competent operators. It is also preferred by insurers because they would not have to review individual companies hire agreements to make sure they were acceptable from an insurance perspective, but would know they were acceptable if they were under CPA conditions. This is not neccessarily due to the time taken to review hire agreements, but it would also negate the possibility of missing important clauses within non standardised hire agreements that could open up potential liability to insurers. When contracts are not under CPA conditions, risk management measures may vary based on the specific terms negotiated between the hiring company and the plant hire company. It is therefore important for due diligence to be conducted to ensure that plant hire companies meet safety and quality standards, including driver competency and equipment maintenance. Contracts may specify the allocation of risks and liabilities between the hiring company and the plant hire company, including responsibilities for accidents, damages, and insurance coverage, and therefore it is imperative to find out the exposures presented by these types of contract conditions.

Training and qualifications will include CPCS and equipment-specific training depending on the types of machinery in use.

The risk management needed will include routine equipment inspections for mechanical issues to prevent equipment failures as well as pre-hire inspections.

Operator training and certification will ensure that operators are competent and knowledgeable. Traffic management plans will mitigate the risks associated with the movement of large machinery on-site.

## Plastering, Drylining and Suspended Ceiling Contractors

Plastering involves the application of plaster to walls and ceilings to create a smooth, finished surface, drylining concerns the installation of plasterboard or drywall to create internal walls, ceilings, or partitions, while suspended ceilings involves installing a secondary ceiling below the main structure to improve aesthetics, acoustics, and accommodate utilities. Often contractors will be involved in all three of these activities, but they may also offer just one of these services.

The skills required for plastering include skimming (a thin layer of plaster applied over plasterboard or other existing surface), rendering (external plastering using sand and cement), and plasterboard application, drylining skills include taping and jointing (a quick and effective alternative to plastering, often used at commercial locations), and for suspended ceilings the skills required will include grid installation, and suspending ceiling tiles or panels.

The equipment used is a variety of mixing, cutting and jointing tools, drywall screw guns and taping knives. The main hazards for these activities are dust exposure, chemical exposure, and working at heights. In terms of training and qualifications, the main courses are City & Guilds plastering courses, National Vocational Qualifications in drylining, and ceiling installer courses.

The risk management undertaken by these contractors must include proper ventilation and handling of materials, use of appropriate PPE including respiratory protection, dust extraction systems to minimise exposure to airborne plaster dust, manual handling training, and fall protection equipment when working at heights.

## Plumbers including Gas Work

Plumbers are responsible for installing, repairing, and maintaining systems that convey fluids—water, gas, or sewage—within buildings. This includes tasks like fitting and repairing pipes, valves, fixtures, and appliances such as water heaters. The skills required are pipefitting, appliance installation, and problem solving by diagnosing and resolving issues.

Modern pipe networks tend to be the 'push fit' plastic piping, while the more traditional pipework is copper. Repairing old pipework can involve soldering, which is more hazardous than repairing or replacing plastic pipes, as heat work creates a greater risk of injury or third party damage. The downside of plastic push fit pipes and pipe fittings, however, is that they have a high propensity of escape of water if they are not fitted correctly. This is particularly common in residential properties, and high rise residential blocks are the most likely to have large escape of water incidents as several storeys can be affected from a single leak. This aspect is a concern to insurers and additional conditions and/or a higher excess are often applied for work in high rise residential properties, so it is important to establish the work locations. Other hazards include exposure to hazardous substances and chemicals, working in confined spaces, and manual handling.

Plumbers will often start their trade under an apprenticeship, although there are also City & Guilds plumbing courses and NVQs.

Their risk management must include proper ventilation, use of PPE, and a hot work permit if any heat work is undertaken.

Leak detection systems are designed to identify and locate leaks in pipelines, tanks, or other containment systems to prevent water damage, environmental contamination, or loss of valuable resources. Leak detection systems may include sensors, probes, alarms, control panels, and communication devices. Advanced systems may also incorporate automated shut-off valves or remote monitoring capabilities.

Contractors involved in large or high end property builds or maintenance sometimes install leak detection systems as part of preventative maintenance strategies to identify potential leaks early, minimising damage and avoiding costly repairs. They must also ensure there is regular maintenance including periodic inspections, testing, and calibration of sensors.

During construction or renovation projects, contractors use temporary leak detection systems to ensure the quality and integrity of plumbing, piping, and HVAC systems.

Contractors sometimes incorporate leak detection systems into risk management plans to mitigate the risk of water damage, mould growth, and structural deterioration. By installing sensors in critical areas susceptible to leaks, such as basements, mechanical rooms, or utility corridors, contractors can detect leaks early and take corrective action.

In the event of a leak or water-related emergency, contractors rely on leak detection systems to facilitate rapid response and minimise damage. Alarms or notifications from the system alert contractors and building managers to the presence of a leak, enabling prompt investigation and intervention.

Whether they use leak detection systems or not, they must ensure that they develop and implement emergency response procedures for addressing leaks, including shut-off procedures, containment measures, and notification protocols.

### *Gas Work*

The Gas Safe Register is the official list of gas engineers legally allowed to work on gas appliances. It replaced CORGI as the gas registration body in 2009. Gas Safe engineers are qualified to work on boilers, gas cookers, fires, and other gas appliances, having gone through specific training and assessments recognised by the Gas Safe Register, which is operated by the relevant Health & Safety Authority in the different areas of the UK. Gas Safe is not a trade association or membership body, but the overseers can carry out monitoring inspections of registered companies, investigate complaints against members for non-compliance of Gas Safety Regulations, or report unauthorised gas work activities to the HSE. Registered contractors are skilled in gas appliance installation and servicing, and gas leak detection. The equipment used consists of gas analysers and detectors, combustion analysers, and gas leak detection equipment.

The main hazards they have to deal with are gas leaks, carbon monoxide poisoning, and faulty installations.

In addition to the mandatory requirement for Gas Safe registration there is also the ACS (Accredited Certification Scheme) which includes assessments covering gas safety and appliance knowledge, and relevant qualifications under City & Guilds, NVQs, or equivalent in gas engineering.

Risk management includes gas safety protocols as detailed in The Gas Safety (Installation and Use) Regulations 1998, including procedures in place for responding to gas emergencies and continuous training to stay updated on the latest gas safety regulations and technologies.

The significance of Gas Safe Registering is:

- Legal compliance: Working on gas appliances without being on the Gas Safe Register is illegal.
- Consumer confidence: Provides assurance to consumers that engineers are qualified and competent.
- Safety assurance: Ensures that gas work is carried out safely, reducing the risk of accidents.

### *Trade Associations*

Chartered Institute of Plumbing and Heating Engineering (CIPHE) The CIPHE is a professional body for the UK plumbing and heating industry. It provides support, training, and representation for plumbing and heating professionals. These engineers can join as members, gaining access to resources, technical advice, and networking opportunities. The CIPHE also offers a range of qualifications and courses to support the professional development of individuals in the plumbing and heating industry. Members are expected to adhere to a code of professional standards, promoting excellence and ethical conduct in the industry.

Membership in professional organisations like the CIPHE can offer a range of benefits including access to industry news, training, and a network of peers. Additionally, membership often reflects a commitment to professionalism and high standards in the field.

British Plumbing Employers' Council (BPEC)
A specialised provider of industry recognised qualifications, assessments, training courses and learning materials, providing evidence of an individual's competence in areas such as installation and maintenance.

Scottish and Northern Ireland Plumbing Employers' Federation (SNIPEF)
SNIPEF is an organisation representing plumbing and heating businesses in Scotland and Northern Ireland. It works to support and represent the interests of plumbing and heating employers. It engages with industry stakeholders, provides resources for professional development, and addresses issues relevant to the plumbing and heating sector.

Membership in SNIPEF provides plumbing and heating companies with a platform to stay informed about industry developments, access training and apprenticeship programs, and participate in initiatives that promote the interests of the sector.

These organisations play crucial roles in supporting and representing the interests of employers in the construction and plumbing sectors. They contribute to the overall well-being of the industries by fostering collaboration, advocating for favourable conditions, and promoting best practices in areas such as safety and professional standards.

## Protective Coating Contractors

Protective coating contractors apply specialised coatings to surfaces for corrosion resistance, fire protection, waterproofing, or aesthetic purposes. They must prepare and clean surfaces before applying paints, sealants, epoxies, etc. Application can involve sprayers, brushes, or rollers.

The main hazards for this activity are exposure to fumes and solvents, working at heights, and potential skin contact with coatings.

Training may include coating application techniques but can also be on the job as an apprentice. They must have an understanding of surface preparation and a knowledge of safety data sheets for coatings.

Their risk management will include proper ventilation during application, use of appropriate PPE including safety gloves and respiratory equipment, and compliance with HSE safety guidelines for spraying.

## Racking Installers

Racking installers specialise in the assembly, installation, and maintenance of storage racks and shelving systems. They are crucial in optimising storage space in warehouses, retail establishments, and industrial facilities. They must have a working knowledge of structural stability and load-bearing capacities, as well as accurate alignment and placement of racks to meet safety and efficiency standards. The equipment used can include power and measuring tools, scissor lifts, boom lifts and cranes.

The main hazards for this activity are work at height, structural failures/collapse, falling objects, manual handling and hot work.

Training can be provided by racking manufacturers on the specific installation requirements for their products, and by SEMA (see below).

Risk management:
- Conducting engineering assessments before installation to ensure that racks meet safety and load-bearing standards.
- Implementing quality control measures during and after installation to verify structural integrity.

- Adhering to the load capacity guidelines provided by rack manufacturers.
- Ensuring that racks are securely anchored to the floor according to manufacturer specifications.
- Full compliance with IPAF and LOLER where applicable.
- Clear communication with crane operators to coordinate the movement of materials and installation activities.

## *Training and Accreditations*

Storage Equipment Manufacturers' Association

SEMA provides guidance and sets industry standards for the design, manufacture, installation, and use of storage equipment, including shelving, racking, and other storage systems.

While SEMA itself doesn't offer a specific accreditation for companies or individuals, it does provide training programs and qualifications related to storage equipment safety. One such qualification is the SEMA Approved Installation Company (SAIC) status.

This is a recognition awarded by SEMA to companies that have demonstrated competence in the installation of storage equipment and systems. This includes racking and shelving commonly used in warehouses and industrial facilities.

The SAIC status signifies that a company has met specific criteria and standards set by SEMA for the safe and proper installation of storage equipment. It helps ensure that installations are carried out by qualified professionals who adhere to industry best practices.

Criteria for SAIC Status:

- The company must have management and supervisory staff with relevant qualifications and experience.
- Installation personnel must undergo training and demonstrate competence in the assembly and installation of storage systems.

- The company must adhere to SEMA's code of practice and guidelines for storage equipment installation.

Benefits of SAIC Status:
- Recognition as a company that meets industry standards for safe and reliable storage equipment installation.
- Confidence for clients and customers that installations are carried out by trained and competent professionals.
- Access to SEMA's resources and updates on industry best practices.

Storage Equipment Installers Registration Scheme Qualification (SEIRS)

This is specific to installers of adjustable pallet racking, and covers various topics relating to the industry - equipment types, installation techniques, safety procedures and industry regulations. There are currently five courses offered by SEMA under the SEIRS umbrella:

- *Foundation Course* (grants an award of a Trainee SEIRS card which is valid for 6 months)
- *Diploma Course* (this is Part 2 following the foundation course and awards the contractors with a Diploma which is valid for 5 years)
- *General Refresher Course* (required to be completed prior to the expiry of the Diploma Card)
- *Supervisors Course* and *Installation Managers Course* (for site supervisors and site managers respectively).

It's important to note that specific details and programs may evolve, and it's recommended to check SEMA's official website for the most up-to-date information on accreditations, qualifications, and training programs related to storage equipment installation.

## Road Works and Traffic Management

Road works encompass construction, repair, and maintenance activities related to roads (both public and private) and highways. This includes tasks such as resurfacing, signage installation, laying of services, and repair of road structures. Traffic management involves planning and implementing measures to control and direct vehicular and pedestrian traffic around construction zones to ensure safety.

Skills include road construction, asphalt laying and groundworks, drainage and erosion control, and traffic management planning. Equipment includes pavers (used to lay asphalt), road rollers, excavators, traffic cones and temporary traffic lights, and signage. The main hazards include those relating to traffic (risks associated with working near moving vehicles, and the potential for incidents where the traffic management procedures are not perfectly placed and timed), excavation and working at depth hazards. The use of diggers also creates the potential for a vibration-related injury to contractors.

The NRSWA (New Roads and Street Works Act) requires that there is a qualified operative on site at all times - see Work at Depth section for further information.

Risk management will include implementing effective traffic management plans including road signage and warnings, use of high-visibility clothing to ensure workers are visible to drivers, and undertaking regular site audits to assess the effectiveness of traffic management measures.

## Roofing Contractors and Solar Panel Installers

Roofers are professionals who install, repair, and maintain roofs on buildings. This includes tasks such as applying roofing materials, repairing leaks, and ensuring the structural integrity of roofs. Solar panel installers specialise in the installation of solar photovoltaic

(PV) systems on roofs to harness solar energy. Hot roofing involves the application of materials like hot bitumen for waterproofing.

Skills involved are roofing techniques, solar panel installation, and hot roofing methods.

Equipment can include roofing materials such as shingles (made of wood, bitumen or metal) or tiles, solar panels, and hot roofing equipment such as blowtorches.

This is a hazardous trade due to the amount of time working at height and the significant risks this involves. Add to that some hot roofing and you have one of the most hazardous activities undertaken by a contractor - heat work at height!

For solar panel installers, there is also the potential for electrical hazards.

Training and qualifications include NVQs in roofing, solar PV installation and working at height.

The risk management required will include suitable fall protection systems such as guardrails, safety nets, or personal fall arrest systems, strict adherence to safe practices during hot roofing installations, and ensuring compliance with electrical safety standards for solar panel installations.

## Scaffolding Contractors

Scaffolding contractors are responsible for the design, erection, maintenance, inspection and dismantling of scaffolding structures. Scaffolding provides temporary support for workers and materials during construction or maintenance activities. It ensures safe access to elevated areas, such as building exteriors, and may involve various types of scaffolding, such as tube and clamp or modular systems.

The skills required include scaffolding design, assembly, and understanding of safety regulations, and the equipment consists of scaffold components (tubes, couplers, boards), hoists, and safety harnesses.

The primary concern when erecting or dismantling scaffolding is falls from height. During the erection stage, when the structure is less likely to be stable and secure, there is an increased risk of falls and collapse of the scaffolding. Other hazards include manual handling from lifting and carrying heavy scaffold components, and third party injury or damage caused by falling scaffolding components.

In terms of training and qualifications there is the CISRS (Construction Industry Scaffolders Record Scheme), and advanced rigging and lifting training for complex scaffolding projects, while the NASC accreditation is considered perhaps the best in the industry in terms of quality and low incident rates - further information below.

The risk management procedures of these contractors must include rigorous safety training for working at height, use of harnesses and helmets (to be inspected before every use and maintained), site specific risk assessments, and regular inspection of scaffolding to ensure structural integrity. Once the structure has been completed, it is up to a Competent Person to ensure that the structure is checked before every use, or every 7 days if not used as regularly. This Competent Person may be someone who has been approved under the CISRS, or someone who has had specific training from the manufacturer/supplier of the scaffolding. It is not unusual for building contractors to erect and maintain their own mobile or tower scaffolding, as long as they have a Competent Person, but for more complex structures, this needs to be carried out by a specialist.

The National Access & Scaffolding Confederation (NASC)
The NASC is a highly regarded trade association for the
scaffolding and access sector, and its membership is comprised of
companies involved in the design, supply, erection, and
dismantling of scaffolding and access equipment. Members must
have an exceptional standard of H&S, and are annually audited by
the NASC to ensure the highest standards are met. They must also
be established a minimum of 2 years before being considered for
membership. H&S must be reviewed and updated annually
including up to date training of fall arrest systems and installing
guardrails safely. Members must complete annual accident returns
to NASC as a full member requirement. (Annual accident reports
are available to read on the NASC website). 99% of NASC
members work without incident, as advised on the NASC website.
Membership alone proves their H&S is to a very high standard due
to the stringent entry requirements.

*Key aspects of NASC membership*
Professional representation:
NASC acts as a collective voice for the scaffolding and access
industry, representing the interests of its members at various levels,
including with government bodies, regulators, and other
stakeholders.
Standards and best practice:

- NASC plays a key role in the development and promotion
  of industry standards, codes of practice, and guidance for
  safe and effective scaffolding operations.
- Members have access to best practice guidance documents
  produced by NASC, contributing to higher safety and
  performance standards.

Training and competency:

- NASC provides training initiatives and resources to enhance the skills and competency of those working in the scaffolding sector.
- Membership involves a commitment to promoting high levels of safety and competence within the industry, aligning with regulatory requirements.

Technical support:

- NASC offers technical support and advice to its members on matters related to scaffolding design, construction, and safety.
- Members receive guidance on regulatory compliance and changes in industry regulations that impact scaffolding operations.

Access to industry updates:

- NASC keeps its members informed about industry news, updates, and relevant changes in legislation that may affect their operations.
- Membership provides opportunities for networking with other professionals in the scaffolding and access industry.

Safety and health initiatives:

- NASC is actively involved in promoting safety initiatives within the scaffolding sector, contributing to the reduction of accidents and improving overall safety performance.
- Members undergo health and safety audits to ensure compliance with industry standards and best practices.

Promotion of industry image:

- NASC engages in public relations activities to promote a positive image of the scaffolding industry and its commitment to safety, quality, and professionalism.

- Being a NASC member enhances a company's reputation within the industry and among clients who prioritise safety and high standards.

Benefits of NASC membership:

- NASC membership is a mark of credibility, signalling a commitment to high standards, safety, and professionalism.
- Members have access to a wealth of resources, including technical guidance, training materials, and industry updates.
- Being part of NASC provides opportunities to connect with other professionals in the scaffolding and access sector.
- Membership ensures that companies stay informed about regulatory changes and maintain compliance with industry standards.
- Insurers look more favourably at NASC scaffolding contractors, and some only cover those with the NASC accreditation due to the high risk nature of the work.

## Shop and Office Fitters

Shop and office fitters are professionals who install and maintain interior fixtures, fittings, and furniture in commercial spaces. Their activities can include carpentry and joinery, plumbing, electrics, plastering, and other ancillary activities as required.

Equipment is usually a mix of hand tools such as saws, drills, screwdrivers, fasteners, and portable woodworking machinery.

The main hazards include manual handling injuries, exposure to adhesives and finishing materials, and use of power tools. There are also the plumbing and electrical hazards that may be present if they are undertaking these activities, but where these activities require any particular accreditation or specialism, for example gas works, then this is generally sub-contracted out to a specialist.

Training is usually by way of a carpentry or joinery apprenticeship, or other construction apprenticeship. Risk management will include safe manual handling practices and proper use of PPE.

## Sign Erectors

Sign erectors are responsible for the installation, maintenance, and sometimes design of various types of signage, including outdoor signs, billboards, and indoor displays, these can be electrical and composed from a variety of materials, such as metal, composite plastic, or wood.

The skills required for this trade include precision in sign installation, knowledge of structural requirements, and electrical wiring for illuminated signs. The equipment can involve mounting brackets, fasteners, electrical wiring and components, lifting and rigging equipment.

Hazards for this activity can include working at heights, electrical hazards, and potential exposure to weather elements. The training required will often involve the understanding of electrical systems, and safety training for working at heights. Their risk management will involve fall protection measures, adherence to electrical safety standards, and regular inspection and maintenance of lifting equiment.

## Steel Erectors and Structural Framing Systems

Steel erectors assemble and install the structural framework of buildings, bridges, or other structures using steel components. Structural Framing Systems (SFS) involves the use of lightweight steel framing for walls and ceilings.

The skills required include interpreting blueprints, welding, and rigging. The equipment used includes cranes, welding equipment, steel framing components.

Hazards associated with this trade include falls and falling objects, as working at heights and handling heavy steel components pose significant risks. Erecting steel structures involves working with heavy loads and machinery which creates hazards such as crushing and pinch points. There is also the concern of unintended structural collapse or heavy machinery overturning. Welding hazards include burns and inhalation of fumes.

Training can be by way of an apprenticeship, and the main qualification is an NVQ in steel erection.

Risk management should include the use of appropriate PPE including safety harnesses, regular equipment inspections, proper rigging and lifting techniques to minimise the risk of dropping materials during installation, and welding safety protocols to ensure proper ventilation.

Good quality steel is vital in construction, due to its strength, durability, and ability to bear heavy loads. Ensuring the quality of steel involves adherence to specific standards and regulations to guarantee safety, performance, and reliability. BS (British Standards) are specific technical specifications and guidelines published by the British Standards Institution (BSI). For construction steel, several BS standards ensure that the steel used is of high quality and fit for purpose. Compliance with these standards ensures consistent quality and performance and reduces the risk of structural failure. It also facilitates adherence to building regulations and codes.

Common BS Standards for steel:

- BS EN 10025: Covers hot-rolled products of structural steels.
- BS 5950: Provides design rules for structural steelwork in building.
- BS 449: Offers specifications for the use of structural steel in building.

- BS EN 1090: CE Marking for structural steel and aluminium.

CE Marking indicates that a product complies with the essential requirements of the relevant European health, safety, and environmental protection legislation. For construction steel, CE marking ensures that the steel meets the necessary European standards, confirming its quality and suitability for use in construction, and is a legal requirement for structural steel products sold in Europe.

Traceability is the ability to track the history, application, or location of an item using recorded data. With construction steel, traceability ensures that each batch of steel can be traced back to its source, production process, and quality checks.

*Concerns with Multi-Storey Buildings*

Using good quality steel is particularly crucial for multi-storey buildings due to the higher loads and stresses involved. It is essential to ensure the steel can:

- support the weight of the structure and its occupants.
- maintain its structural integrity under fire conditions.
- withstand long-term stresses and environmental factors without significant degradation.

The manufacture of structural steel is a higher liability risk than just cutting and bolting together pre-made components where there is full traceability back to the manufacturer. The potential for large losses is significant particularly for multi-storey buildings, and some insurers may limit what they can write in this field, and only where the steel is made to British Standards and is CE marked.

## Stonemasons

Stonemasons work with natural and artificial stone to create structures, monuments, and decorative features. Skills involve carving and shaping stone, precision in detailing and finishing, and knowledge of different types of stone. The equipment used will include hand tools (chisels, hammers), power tools (grinders, saws), and lifting and handling equipment.

The hazards of this trade include injuries from hand and power tools, respiratory issues from stone dust, and manual handling injuries.

Training for this trade will be via a stonemasonry apprenticeship or vocational training, and will include learning about safety regulations and technical (and artistic) proficiency in stonework. Standard risk management will be required - Proper use of PPE, dust control measures, and regular equipment maintenance.

## Tilers

Tiling involves the installation of tiles on surfaces such as floors, walls, and countertops. This can include ceramic, porcelain, or natural stone tiles. Precision in tile placement and knowledge of adhesives and grouting will be required.

Hazards will include dust and fumes, manual handling, and working at heights.

Tiling apprenticeships will cover all the skills required, and will provide a working knowledge of safety protocols. Risk management will include proper handling of tools, protection against dust (for the contractors, third parties, and surrounding property), and workplace safety including manual handling training.

# Different Perspectives: Interviews with Industry Professionals

## Interview with an underwriter

**How long have you been in the insurance industry?**
Too long!! I started working in insurance when I was at University in a call centre and went into broking when I left. I moved between broking and underwriting for a few years and finally decided that underwriting was where I wanted to grow my career; I've been here ever since. A total of 23 years now.

**What do you do?** I'm currently an Underwriting Manager.

**In your experience, what are the most common hazards or challenges specific to the construction industry that underwriters need to consider?**
One of the most well known hazards – and for good reason! – is falls from height and these certainly make most of the headlines, but one of the most common causes I see in claims is people taking shortcuts around Health and Safety. There are a number of challenges in contracting trades and particularly on somewhere like a building site which is naturally a very busy working environment so it's important that everyone follows the guidance. Good Health and Safety, whilst not the most exciting of topics for clients, really does prevent injury and saves peoples lives, and underwriters need to make sure that their clients have a good grasp of this and are implementing good working practices on site.

**What factors do you consider most critical in determining risk acceptance for construction businesses?**

For me there are two factors. Firstly, does the broker understand what they are presenting to you? Have they included Health and Safety information, working practices where height and depth work are undertaken, information on hot work? A good broker presentation with sufficient information means that they have asked of the client, and understood, the risk being presented. Secondly, does the client have these sound working practices and are they borne out in the claims experience?

**In your opinion, do you think that commercial brokers and underwriters have a good knowledge of the construction industry, and if not, why do you think this is?**
I think some do and where these is good knowledge,  those brokers (and underwriters) tend to be the ones who specialise in construction. It is quite a complex product with a lot of variances – no two builders are going to present the same risk to an underwriter – and so, certainly from an underwriting perspective, it's really important that there's continuous professional development in this area.

**Given the evolving nature of the construction industry, how do you stay updated on emerging risks and trends?**
HSE is a really great source of information on the changing rules within the construction industry. I've mentioned builders a couple of times but 'construction' covers a wide range of industries so it's also really important that we have a good knowledge of all trades and what risks they can entail.

**Have there been any memorable cases you have come across, either positive or negative?**
Well, I mentioned above taking shortcuts on building sites and one of my most memorable claims was someone who decided to take a

shortcut between two lots of scaffolding whilst two storeys up. I'll leave it to your imagination as to how that one ended!

**Any last thoughts?**
Construction is a really interesting part of insurance for me - challenging sometimes but always varied! Top tip is keep on top of your knowledge, whichever part of the insurance industry you work in.

## Interview with a broker

**How long have you been in the insurance industry?**
33 years, always in the broking industry.

**What does your role entail?**
I'm an MD of a small brokerage where I manage several hundred clients. I have previously been involved with sales, team management, marketing and everything in between.

**In your experience, what are the most common hazards or challenges specific to the construction industry that brokers need to consider?**
First and foremost, I look to help them with their business, advise where I can and refer them to specialists when I can't – whether that is in relation to Finance, or referral to an External H&S Consultant.
A specific challenge for brokers is that a lot of clients are remote, as there is no requirement for a premises visit for construction businesses – their work is in different locations and not premises based.
Depth is a massive hazard – more of a concern than height and heat work in my opinion.

Other activities include anything to do with asbestos, demolition, environmental risk, but these are less frequent.

Ground remediation can cause problems – if the Environmental Agency get involved costs can be exhaustive.

A general builder that might turn his hand to a bit of plumbing, or a bit of electrical wiring, so we need to ask those questions about their specific activities that might be more hazardous or specialised than we were aware of.

I'm always interested in the workforce, as recruitment and retention is a big issue and retention rates are important. Do they have LOSC and BFSC? I explain to them the difference, do they use LOSC and BFSC that they have worked with for many years? Communication systems for safe systems of work are key – They may have all the necessary steps in place, but how do they communicate it to all contractors across all sites?

**What factors do you consider most critical in determining risk acceptance for construction businesses?**

Moral hazard is a huge issue – I won't be dealing with an individual or a company that does not have H&S or does not want to be asked the H&S questions.

With the many years experience I have, sometimes I reframe the question – 'If you want a low premium, you need to have good risk management, its not just about claims experience, and if you want to keep your business in business, then re-think how you want to answer those questions.'

I will only work with people who are serious about protecting their business.

**In your opinion, do you think that commercial brokers and underwriters have a good knowledge of the construction industry, and if not, why do you think this is?**

Its patchy, those that specialise in them will have a good knowledge of H&S and regulatory requirements. But even they have a limitation of knowledge of what can kill a business – Finance, lengthy contract disputes, the operational risk, etc. Underwriters and claims handlers have been great teachers on the subject, I have questioned them over the years on their decisions – like why they consider something is an issue that I haven't considered or come across before, such as emerging risks.

I think this gap in knowledge is due to training, money, and leadership, all are key.

A broker, for example, has to hit sales, leadership may not be good and advice is limited. So with a minimum amount of resource, training and time, they just have a standard form to fill out, and that's where they will miss pertinent information as they don't know what else to ask.

People don't know any better – they don't set their bar high enough.

**Given the evolving nature of the construction industry, how do you stay updated on emerging risks and trends?**

As I mentioned before, talking to underwriters and asking questions has been extremely useful in gaining knowledge, and I would definitely recommend this – if you don't understand a term or a decision, then ask for an explanation.

I also read insurance contracts – these can be very different across different providers, particularly for emerging risks. Then I will ask underwriters to explain any particular clauses or exclusions that I don't fully understand.

**Have there been any memorable cases you have come across, either positive or negative?**

I know of a case of poor broking. It was a client with no EL cover, and a contractor fell through a roof and broke both legs. There was audio of the sales call, and the sales person established it was a single person business with no contractors and no employees so decided it was ok for no EL cover. However the person that was on the other end of the phone was not paying attention on the call, they were distracted by instructing someone and operating their own plant, and therefore was not a sole trader. The claim was repudiated as there was no EL cover in force. It was a lack of common sense.

There was another situation that turned out more positively. There was a contractor that had a tools and material theft, a bit of a security issue across multiple sites as they didn't know who was there and when.

I advised them to install turnstiles with biometric access to an anteroom, where H&S and PPE was checked, so that they then knew who was on site and when, and this improved the safety of the site, there was less theft, and it actually reduced the contract works premium due to this additional security.

**Any last thoughts?**

There are a few points that brokers need to be aware of.
Your client should want something more than just a cheap price.
It should bother any broker when they have a client that has an uninsured loss. But we can't always know every single little activity they do – I once had a client who was a telegraph pole erector who used a chainsaw on a cherry picker for cutting branches. There was no way I could have expected that!

You need to be pushy – contractors need to tell brokers exactly what they do and what they use. My advice – when you think you've asked everything, put the kettle on and ask some more.

## Interview with a plumber

**How long have you been in the construction industry?**
20 years

**What does your job entail?**
I'm a plumbing and heating engineer so I undertake a wide variety of contracts - bathroom renovations, boiler installation, emergency maintenance on heating systems - and anything to do with hot water systems, gas central heating and water pipes. I do occasionally do heat work using blow torches.

**Where do you undertake these contracts?** Mostly residential, work on large estates, and commercial such as schools, but no industrial work.

**What are the types of hazards you face when undertaking a contract?**
Escape of water if pipes are knocked, use of heat, finding asbestos, long term physical issues due to kneeling in cramped spaces.

**What risk management steps do you take?**
Its very much an automatic pilot thing now that has come from years of experience. I do risk assessments and method statements on the job, from experience I know what needs to be done in order to reduce the risk of incidents happening. The main things are water shut off and removing water using a wet and dry hoover to

avoid leakage during work, protecting furniture and the surrounding area, and using PPE. Those that work with me and for me must also use PPE.

**Have you had any incidents over the years which you have had to claim for?**
I can honestly say no I have not.

**What are your thoughts on risk management and keeping documentation - Is it a help or a hindrance?**
Its definitely a help, it makes it easier whilst working to go back over any details, and it makes sense that regulators and insurance companies want this in place.

**Any thoughts on the fact that insurers treat plumbing as a trade to be cautious of due to large escape of water incidents?**
I think they are right, the main issues seems to be project management companies who have no experience in the trade and just get anyone in to do the job, and not necessarily very well.

# Construction Insurance: Policy Cover and Exclusions

### What is liability insurance for contractors?

**Employers Liability insurance** is designed to cover compensation and legal costs in case an employee brings a claim against their employer due to work-related incidents and injuries.

**Public Liability insurance** comes into play when third parties—customers, visitors, or passers-by—sustain injury or property damage due to a contractors activities. It safeguards individuals or businesses against legal claims and costs.

### What are the main exclusions under liability insurance?

*Faulty workmanship* - Excludes the cost of rectifying defective workmanship, although subsequent damage caused by defective work might be covered.

*Professional services* - Claims arising from professional services provided by the contractor although these can be covered under a separate professional indemnity policy.

*Pollution and environmental damage* - Claims related to pollution or environmental damage, unless caused by a sudden, identifiable, unexpected and unintended event.

*Intentional acts* - Damage or injury resulting from deliberate, wilful, or intentional acts by the contractor or their employees.

*Hazardous locations* - Work conducted at hazardous locations such as airports, railways, chemical plants, and offshore installations may be excluded unless specifically covered.

*Hazardous work activities* - High-risk activities like demolition, asbestos removal, and work at significant heights or depths without proper coverage or endorsements.

*Asbestos-related claims* - Any claims related to the handling, removal, or exposure to asbestos. Asbestos is a common insurance policy exclusion under PL, however it cannot be specifically excluded under EL. For this reason, many insurers will not cover a business which has a likelihood of coming across asbestos and dealing with it themselves.

## What is Contractors All Risks insurance for contractors?
### Contract Works

This insurance provides coverage for construction projects specified in a contract. It is designed to protect against the risk of damage to the materials and equipment. The contract could be for a new build of a multi storey building, or a large contract involved with the construction of major roadworks. The insurance can be arranged for a specific contract - generally for large or lengthy outliers to a companies normal contracts - or on a blanket basis for all the contracts within a 12 month period if the size and duration is normally uniform.

The policy is commonly issued under the name of the Employer/Principal and the Contractor, and if not explicitly within the name of the Insured, then as a minimum both parties are covered under a specific Clause, as required by the contract conditions. Often for an annual policy this is the way cover is provided, as it would be impossible (and messy) to name every party to every contract within the year as the Insured.

This insurance typically covers loss or damage to the works and materials used for the construction project, whilst in transit (other than sea and air transit) or on site.

Policy liability is limited to the sum insured, which is based on the Estimated Original Contract Price. This is generally defined within the policy wording as the estimated valuation or contract price at the start of the contract. This tends to be underestimated so insurers usually allow a 15-25% uplift to compensate for this and the unexpected additional costs that may be added on during the course of the contract. This is not normally free of charge - once the final contract price or a higher turnover is known a charge is applied.

Cover is on an All Risks basis (hence the name) so the common perils such as fire, flood, theft, vandalism, and accidental damage are included.

Coverage usually begins from delivery of materials and continues until handover to the employer, plus a maintenance period. This is where the contractor is still responsible for rectifying defects where the cause was before the maintenance period i.e. before the handover and when they were still responsible for the Works. This is typically twelve months but longer periods are sometimes requested for an additional charge depending on the terms of the contract with the Employer.

An important point to note is that the limit of cover ties in directly with the contract price stated in the contract. Sometimes, an Employer will request cover for a higher limit to be provided and stated on the policy documents, however there would be no cover for this in practice, as cover is limited to the Estimated Original Contract Price plus the uplift agreed. Underwriters will highlight this to brokers, as the client will be paying an additional premium for a cover that is not provided.

**Own Plant**

Cover for own plant ensures that the essential tools and machinery necessary for construction projects are protected from unforeseen

223

events. It typically covers physical damage to the equipment, including accidental damage, fire, theft, vandalism, and malicious damage, whilst adjacent to or on site, whilst in transit there and back, or when not in use back at the contractors premises. It is based on the Sum Insured provided, and is normally on an indemnity basis, so rather than the 'new for old' reinstatement basis, the settlement will be based on the value of the item at the time of the damage or loss.

Following the COVID-19 pandemic, there was a spike in construction plant fires, the causes often being failure of hydraulic hoses (due to fluid leakage or running on low fluid levels) or electrical faults, as the plant were being worked harder to try and make up for the project delays.

**Hired In Plant**

Cover for hired in plant is the same as own plant in terms of loss or damage and the locations covered, but can also be on a legal liability basis under the terms of the hire contract for loss or damage to the plant, and for ongoing hiring charges until the plant is either repaired or replaced. There is often a clause within the policy wording covering continuing hiring charges, but can sometimes be subject to:

- a maximum sum insured (e.g. a maximum limit of £25,000 any one hire agreement)
- a maximum indemnity period (e.g. cover limited to 90 days after the damage/loss occurred), or
- a time excess (e.g. excluding the first 48 hours following the damage/loss)

Sometimes cover is not subject to any of these conditions, and the policy wording refers only to the responsibilities required under the hire agreement. Therefore it is imperative that insurers settle claims for loss or damage to hired in plant as quickly as possible to reduce the amount payable under this clause.

There may also be coverage for additional expenses incurred due to the loss or damage of hired equipment, such as hiring replacement equipment or transportation costs.

Cover for electrical or mechanical breakdown is included only as far as the hire agreement states is the responsibility of the entity hiring the plant.

There is no cover for plant purchased under a leasing or hire purchase agreement (as this should be insured as own plant).

Hired In Plant cover may contain certain exclusions or limitations, such as exclusions for wear and tear, gradual deterioration, mechanical breakdown, or damage resulting from negligence or misuse.

Exclusions may also apply to certain types of equipment or specific high-risk activities, such as underwater operations, demolition work, or hazardous material handling.

## Employees' Tools

Employees' personal tools and effects coverage provides insurance protection for the personal belongings, tools, equipment, and effects owned by employees and used in the course of their work on construction sites.

This coverage typically extends to loss or damage to employees' personal property caused by insured perils, including theft, fire, vandalism, accidental damage, and other covered events.

Employees' personal tools and effects, such as hand tools, power tools, protective gear, clothing, and personal belongings, are covered while they are on-site or in transit to and from the construction site.

Claims settlement is based on the market value at the time of the loss and not on a reinstatement as new basis.

The standard limits of coverage for Employees' Personal Tools and Effects may vary depending on the insurance policy and insurer. However, coverage limits are typically set based on the aggregate value of employees' personal property and/or a predetermined limit per employee.

Common exclusions include motor vehicles, money, and jewellery, as well as the standard exclusions of wear and tear and mechanical or electrical breakdown or failure.

**What are the cover highlights under CAR insurance?**

There are a number of useful covers under CAR insurance that insurers often advertise as the main benefits of their policy, however most of these are industry standard.

*Additional Interests*

This provision allows other parties with an insurable interest in the project (contractors, subcontractors, or employers) to be included as insured under the policy, to the extent required by the contract conditions.

*Continuing Hire Charges*

This covers the costs incurred for the continued hire of plant and equipment while it is being repaired or replaced due to damage to the HIP or due to breakdown of the HIP caused by negligence or misuse of employees.

*Immobilised Plant*

This covers the cost of recovering or repairing plant and machinery that has become immobilised (e.g., stuck or broken down) on the construction site.

*Off-site Storage*

This covers materials, equipment, and components stored off-site that are intended for use in the construction project, and there will usually be an inner limit applied.

*Re-drawing Plans or Documents*
This covers the costs associated with re-writing or re-drawing architectural or engineering plans and documents that are lost or damaged. This will normally be subject to an inner limit.

*Speculative Builds*
This provides coverage for construction projects that are started without a specific buyer or tenant in place at the outset, meaning the building is constructed 'on spec' in the hope of selling or leasing it upon completion. There is usually a limited timescale applied to the cover, for example 90 days after practical completion.

*Show Properties*
This covers properties that are built and used as show homes or display units to demonstrate the design and build quality to potential buyers. This will often include the contents. There are usually some caveats to this cover, for example ensuring water systems are drained during the colder months and adequately secured when unattended. Cover will expire shortly after practical completion of the contract, the exact number of days may differ between insurers.

Other useful covers include:
Loss of keys
Incidental hiring of plant
Expediting expenses


**What are the main exclusions under CAR insurance?**
*Defective workmanship* - Costs associated with correcting defective workmanship or materials, though resultant damage might be covered - see section below on Defective Exclusions.
*Wear and Tear* - Loss or damage due to normal wear and tear, gradual deterioration, or corrosion.

*Existing Property* - Damage to existing structures or property unless specifically covered by an extension to the policy.

*Financial Loss* - Pure financial losses not resulting from physical damage, such as loss of profit or delays in project completion. This cover can often be arranged as an extension or under a separate FL policy.

*Hazardous locations* - Work conducted at particularly hazardous locations (e.g., bridges, tunnels, chemical plants or nuclear facilities) unless specifically covered by the policy.

### Defective Exclusions

The idea behind these Exclusions is to avoid underwriting the risk of a contractors design and workmanship - these are more appropriately covered under a PI policy. There are 5 Exclusions, although DE1 and DE2 are such broad exclusions that they are not normally used or agreed upon within the requirements for insurance, and DE3 is used as standard within policy wordings.

In simple terms, Defective Exclusion 3 (DE3) refers to a specific exclusion found in many insurance policies for contractors. This exclusion means that the insurance policy will not cover the cost of fixing any defects in the construction work itself. However, if those defects cause damage to other parts of the property that are free of defects, this cover is not excluded.

For example, if a contractor installs a faulty roof that leaks, the insurance won't pay to replace or repair the roof. But if the defective roof causes water damage to the interior of the building, cover for this would not be excluded.

So DE3 essentially says: "We won't pay to fix your mistakes, but we might pay for the damage your mistakes cause."

DE4 is a type of exclusion where the policy does not cover the cost to repair or replace component parts that are defective, but will cover other parts or items of the property which are free of defect and damaged as a result of the defect.

Example: If a contractor installs a roof that later leaks, and it is found that the cause was due to a defective batch of tiles, DE4 won't cover the cost to fix the defective tiles, but it will cover damage to the interior of the building or other parts of the roof that are not defective, that have been damaged as a result of the defect (e.g. the waterproof membrane underneath).

DE5 provides the widest coverage. It covers not only the damage caused by the defective work or materials but also the cost to repair or replace the defective part itself. Essentially, it offers full coverage for both the defect and the resulting damage.

Example: Using the same defective roof scenario, DE5 would cover the cost to fix the defective roof including the defective parts and also pay for the repairs to the interior damage caused by the leak.

*Availability in the market*

DE4 is available in the market, but it is a common opinion that for the additional costs and large excess involved, it does not provide much wider cover than DE3 and is not often requested.

DE5 provides the most comprehensive coverage but is less commonly available. When it is available, it usually comes at a higher premium and a very large co-insurance excess because it offers broader protection, covering both the defect and any resulting damage.

## JCT Clause 6: Insurance of the Works and Liabilities

The contract will specify whether the employer or the contractor is responsible for arranging the insurance. The choice often depends on the type of contract and the specific arrangements agreed upon by the parties. Whilst each JCT form is similar, there are some differences, and the example below is specifically from the JCT Standard Building Contract.

The party responsible for arranging the insurance must provide evidence of the insurance cover to the other party, ensuring transparency and compliance with the contractual obligations. The responsible party must select an appropriate insurance policy that meets the specific needs and risks of the construction project. In each case, there must be a Joint Names Policy. However in practice this is often covered under the policy wording as a Clause, extending cover to the Employer or Contractor as required under contract conditions (this can be under the liability and the CAR sections of the policy wording). The reason for this is that a building firm is likely to have multiple contracts ongoing at the same time, and this Joint Names requirement would necessitate separate insurance policies for each contract which is impractical and costly. Joint Names Policies are more common and more practical when a contract is insured on an individual policy anyway (perhaps because of size and/or duration being outside the scope of an annual policy).

There are three insurance options under JCT as follows:

*Insurance of the Works by the Contractor (Option A)*\*

This option requires the contractor to insure the works against all risks from the start of the works until practical completion, and must cover the full reinstatement value of the works, including materials, labour, and professional fees.

*Insurance of the Works by the Employer (Option B)*\*

This option requires the employer to insure the works as per the requirements under Option A.

*Insurance of Existing Structures and Contents, and the works (Option C)*

This option deals with the insurance of existing structures and their contents when construction works are being carried out on or adjacent to them. As well as the works, the insurance must cover the existing structures and contents against loss or damage caused by the contractor's activities. Coverage should extend for the duration of the works. The employer is responsible for this insurance, ensuring that the existing property is protected during the construction process.

*These options are for new builds, Option C is for work on existing buildings.

By specifying who is responsible for each type of insurance, the clauses help prevent disputes and ensure that all parties understand their obligations.

In summary, the main points of Clause 6 cover the following:

*Clause 6.1* requires the contractor to indemnify the employer 'for any Expense, Liability, Loss, Claim, or Proceedings in respect of personal injury or death caused by the carrying out of the works except due to any act or neglect of the employer'.

*Clause 6.2* requires that the contractor indemnifies the employer in respect of any property damage to the works, but excludes the existing structures and damage to the building materials. The liability is only in respect of property damage caused by negligence, breach of statutory duty, omission or default.

*Clause 6.4* mandates that the contractor obtain and maintain insurance covering the liabilities outlined in clauses 6.1 and 6.2. The JCT contract requires the contractor to have both third-party and employer's liability insurance. The policy must include an 'Indemnity to Principal' clause to fulfill the contractual obligation to indemnify the employer, and this is standard within most policy wordings. While the contractor can choose how to secure their liability insurance, they must provide evidence of both policy coverage and premium payment upon request.

Under the JCT contract, the minimum EL coverage is £5 million (insurance companies tend to provide £10M as standard), and the minimum PL coverage is specified in the contract. Contractors should understand that although the JCT contract specifies a limit for the required insurance, the indemnity they provide to the employer is unlimited. Even if the insurance coverage falls short, the contractor must still indemnify the employer, and therefore it is prudent for contractors to negotiate a limit to their indemnity under the contract.

## Clause 6.5.1

Clause 6.5.1 (formerly 21.2.1), Non-Negligence Insurance, and Party Wall Liability Insurance refer to essentially the same type of coverage under different terminologies.

This cover is designed to protect the Employer against third-party claims for damage to property that occur as a result of construction activities, even when the contractor is not negligent. This is crucial in situations where the construction work affects neighbouring properties or shared structures like party walls.

Normally, this requires to be set up in Joint Names of the Employer and Contractor, even though the Contractor cannot benefit from the cover themselves.

This covers vibration, removal or weakening of support, subsidence, collapse, heave, or lowering of groundwater that might inadvertently affect adjacent properties or shared walls, whilst undertaking a building contract.

Example Scenario:

A contractor is conducting excavation work near an adjacent building. Cracks appear in the neighbouring property's walls. An engineering inspection found that the cause was vibration by the works. Generally this does not result in significant cracking to buildings, and was not a result of the contractors negligence.

The affected property owner makes a claim for the damage, and indemnity is provided under the JCT 6.5.1 policy.

The cost of these claims can be significant, particularly in comparison to the premiums paid, and often insurers will not consider providing this cover unless they are also providing cover for the underlying PL risk. There is a benefit to having both of these covers written by the same insurer, in that it will avoid any potential disputes about whether the damage was caused by negligence or not - the sole insurer will be responsible for paying the claim. 6.5.1 will be cheaper in rural locations with no surrounding properties compared to crowded city centres.

**Policy Conditions**

In addition to the cover section and the exclusions applicable, there will also be some conditions that must be adhered to in order for the policy to respond in the event of an insurable incident.
These tend to fall under a heading of 'Reasonable Precautions' or similar.
They require that:
- The property insured is maintained and safeguarded against loss or damage as far as is practical (reasonable steps).
- All relevant Government laws and regulations are complied with, including statutory inspections and Health and Safety.
- Regular inspections are undertaken and any identified hazards are addressed promptly.

This can be broken down further to more specific requirements of what would be considered reasonable precautions:
- Adequate site security to be implemented and maintained.
- Fire protections to be installed, serviced and maintained in line with legal requirements.
- Waste materials must be cleared and removed from site daily.
- Immobilisers on plant must be used if installed.

## The Importance of Checking Policy Cover

Companies need to be aware of the specific cover and exclusions on their own policies to manage their risks effectively. What is important to remember is that most insurance policies follow a standard form, however the exact wordings may differ significantly.

If their operations include activities that are excluded, they must inform their broker or insurance company to advise them and request for cover to be considered. Where the primary insurer cannot cover these activities, the company will have to purchase additional specialised insurance that covers those specific risks.

# Construction Claims

## Types of Liability Claims

Liability claims can arise from various situations - diseases, injuries and fatal accidents to employees, sub contractors, or third parties, and third party property damage. The policy will likely respond where it is proven that the incident arose from the actions or negligence of the insured party. The policy may specify the circumstances under which coverage applies, and exclusions may exist for intentional acts or certain high-risk activities. There will be financial impacts such as compensation claims, medical expenses and long term care costs, and legal costs. There will also possibly be a reputational impact, such as damage to the company's reputation and potential regulatory scrutiny and investigations from the HSE.

Let's consider each of the claim types in turn.

## Disease Claims

Claims arise when an employee or, less commonly a third party, develops a disease due to exposure to hazardous substances or conditions at the construction site. Examples include asbestosis from asbestos exposure, silicosis from inhaling silica dust, or skin conditions from chemical exposure. Disease claims can emerge long after the initial exposure, complicating liability and compensation processes. Policies may include specific language regarding the types of diseases covered, and limited exclusions may apply. The relevant cover section would be EL, or PL for third parties.

## Injuries or Fatalities of Employees or LOSC

Claims arise when an employee is injured or killed while performing their job duties. Examples include falls from height, equipment-related injuries, or exposure to hazardous substances. The relevant policy cover would be EL.

## Injuries or Fatalities of Third Parties or BFSC

Claims arise when a non-employee (e.g., visitors, subcontractors, or the general public) is injured or killed on or around the construction site. For example, a passerby is injured by falling debris or a visitor slipping on-site. The relevant cover section is PL.

## Third Party Property Damage

Claims arise when construction activities cause damage to property not owned by the construction company, this can include damage to buildings, vehicles, or other tangible assets. For example, damage to a neighbouring building during excavation or accidental damage to a client's property. Liability insurance may cover the cost of repairing or replacing the damaged property. Intentional damage will be excluded, and coverage may depend on the insured's legal liability for the damage. The basis of claims settlement will be indemnity. The policy will have limits on the amount of coverage available for property damage, and deductibles may apply. The relevant cover is PL.

## Types of Damages for Injuries and Diseases

When an injury, fatality or disease claim is made, compensation is typically divided into two main categories:

*Special Damages*

These are quantifiable financial losses incurred as a result of the injury or disease.

For example:

- Medical expenses: Costs for hospital stays, surgeries, medications, and rehabilitation.
- Loss of earnings: Compensation for lost income due to inability to work.
- Travel expenses: Costs for traveling to and from medical appointments.
- Care costs: Expenses for any care or assistance required due to the injury or disease.

*General Damages*

These are non-quantifiable losses that compensate for the injury, fatality or disease itself and its impact on the individual's or their families life. For example:

- Pain and suffering: Compensation for physical pain and emotional distress.
- Loss of amenity: Compensation for loss of enjoyment of life or the inability to participate in activities previously enjoyed.
- Psychological impact: Compensation for mental health issues resulting from the injury or disease.

Future Losses

This could include reduction in earnings, or if the claim is for a fatal accident, it could be the sustained financial loss faced by the dependant due to the death of the deceased.

Future losses are typically calculated using actuarial methods and consider factors such as life expectancy, inflation, potential wage growth, and the discount rate (i.e. the Ogden rate - see below) to account for the investment returns on the lump sum awarded.

By including future losses in compensation, the legal system aims to provide a comprehensive financial remedy that addresses both immediate and long-term needs of the injured party or their dependants.

**Ogden/Personal Injury Discount Rate**

The Ogden discount rate (ODR), or Personal Injury Discount Rate (PIDR), is used to calculate the lump sum compensation for future financial losses in personal injury and fatal accident claims. This rate adjusts the lump sum to account for the return on investment that the claimant can expect from investing the lump sum over their lifetime.

A lower Ogden rate increases the compensation amount, as it assumes lower returns on investment, necessitating a larger lump sum to meet future needs. Under the Civil Liability Act 2018, the government is required to review the Ogden rate every five years, with the Lord Chancellor now having to determine the rate by January 2025. The discount rate is different for Scotland and Northern Ireland, while England and Wales have the same rate. After 15 years of no change to the discount rate, in 2016 it was changed from 2.5% to -0.75%, which meant a huge increase in liability claims costs. The last rate review in 2019 amended the rate to -0.25% which still meant a significant impact on previous liability claim costs and as a result insurers had to increase their rates in order to compensate for the increased claims costs. The Ogden rate is a consistent component of claims costs, and time will tell how the next rate review will impact the cost of liability claims.

**Types of CAR Claims**

The types of CAR claims are relatively straightforward, and consist of:

- Damage to the construction works, on-site materials, and temporary structures.
- Damage or theft of construction plant and equipment either owned by the contractor or hired for the project.

Theft of plant is the most frequent type of claim, and over £100m worth of plant is stolen each year.

The policy cover is generally on an All Risks basis, and the Basis of Settlement is indemnity rather than reinstatement. This means the insurer covers the cost of repairing or replacing the damaged property to its condition before the loss. The payout is based on the current value of the damaged property, considering depreciation and wear and tear. Certain items may have sub-limits, capping the maximum payout for specific types of damage or losses.

Claims are generally dealt with by paying a monetary amount to repair or replace the works, or for the damaged or stolen plant and equipment.

The specifics of coverage can vary based on the terms and conditions of the policy, including any exclusions or limitations. It's crucial for policyholders to thoroughly understand their liability insurance policy, including the specific coverages, limits, and any exclusions that may apply. Additionally, prompt reporting of incidents to the insurance provider and cooperation during the claims process are essential to ensure that the insurance company can effectively assess and address the claim.

**Increasing Costs of Materials and Labour, and Project Delays**
Claims costs have been on an upward trajectory for years. Several global and regional events have significantly impacted the costs of construction materials and labour, as well as caused project delays. Key factors include the COVID-19 pandemic, the war in Ukraine, and the global recession.

*COVID-19 Pandemic*
While most construction markets have recovered in terms of output since the end of the pandemic, there still remains a residual issue

with supply chain and labour shortages, delays in procurement, and the price inflation of materials.

The cost of materials is beginning to stabilise as global demand has slowed as a result of high inflation and interest rates, and this has prevented further price acceleration. Contractors are now considering supply chain disruptions as a serious factor to consider when planning projects, and in addition to relying more on domestically sourced materials, many have chosen to purchase materials in advance. Whilst this often means a negative cashflow, this is offset by cost savings and the unknown exposures to future shortages.

Labour costs have continued to increase due to a combination of
a) an increasing labour demand - for example, for housing projects to address the housing crisis.
b) a reduction in labour supply - although the workforce has recovered from the effects of losses during the pandemic, there is a lingering challenge, namely more skilled labourers retiring and less entering the construction industry, and new initiatives have been set up to try and reduce the skill gap. However, years of experience lost cannot be replaced by young recruits, and new technology can only impact productivity to a certain degree.

*War in Ukraine*

Ukraine and Russia are significant exporters of raw materials such as metals and energy resources. The conflict has disrupted these exports, causing continuing shortages and price increases for materials like bricks, steel, aluminium and timber. The war has led to volatility in global energy markets, driving up the cost of fuel and energy-intensive materials. This has had a cascading effect on the cost of manufacturing and transporting construction materials.

*Global Recession*

The economic downturn has lead to reduced industrial activity, affecting the production and supply of construction materials.

Manufacturers have cut back on output, which has lead to shortages.

Recession-related inflation has increased the cost of materials. As prices rise across various sectors, construction materials have become more expensive.

The effect on labour has been significant - skilled labour demands higher pay due to increased competition among employers for a smaller pool of qualified workers.

Economic uncertainty can lead to job instability, affecting the availability and reliability of the workforce.

Project delays can be caused by financing challenges. Recession often leads to tighter credit conditions and reduced availability of financing for construction projects, which may be delayed or canceled due to lack of funding.

**Elevated Claims Costs and Gaps in Coverage**

Contract works insurance typically operates with a limit of indemnity rather than being subject to the average (underinsurance) clause. This limit is calculated by adding an escalator clause uplift, usually 15-20%, onto the original contract value. However, due to the significant increases in material costs driven by factors such as the COVID-19 pandemic, the war in Ukraine, and the global recession, this escalator provision may be insufficient. As a result, the insurance may not cover the full cost of a claim, potentially leaving a gap in coverage.

# Conclusion

Well that's about it from me!

I truly hope that this book has been useful in grasping the fundamentals of the construction industry and some of the basic insurance covers available. It would be impossible to cover everything in one book, but if there is any topic you would like to know more about, I would encourage you to do your own research. There is a wealth of knowledge available on the website, and I have included my list of References on the next page where there is plenty of additional information to get you started. The aim of this book was to bring together the most relevant facts relating to the construction and insurance industries, to tie them together to allow insurance professionals to have a better understanding of the combined topic all in one place, and to make sense of the terminology that they perhaps had heard before but never fully understood.

If I can give you any advice when it comes to considering a business and its associated hazards and risks, even what appear to be the most complex businesses, it would be to break it down. Don't become overwhelmed, step back, and look at what they do day to day. The physical activity, the location, the process. We have a wonderful companion to help us that we didn't have in its current state 20 years ago - Google. You can learn so much from professional sites about trades and regulations, and social media will show you videos of activities, and perhaps a different side to the business you were intending to write!

If the client has a website, look at it. It might help explain activities, give you a glimpse of some of their recent contracts, or provide you with a list of their accreditations. It may also highlight some interesting activities that had not been mentioned. If you are an underwriter, speak to the broker, if you are a broker, speak to the client - this will not only educate you on the clients business but it will also help you build a working relationship. The best brokers will appreciate a conversation about their client, and a client will appreciate their broker taking an interest in the best way to protect their business, so you can all learn along the way.

Once you have understood what the contractor actually does, you need to think about the 'bad stuff', the things that could happen or go wrong i.e. Working at height - falling, working with heat - fire. You then need to consider what they would need to do in order to minimise the risks involved, and ensure they are implemented i.e. fall minimisation methods for work at height, ensuring the area is clear of combustibles when undertaking heat work. I may be using very simple and basic examples here, but the principle remains the same regardless of the complexity of the contract.

The HSE website is a fantastic source of information and I would highly recommend adding it to your favourites as an insurance professional. There is also much to learn from HSE investigation reports following incidents that have resulted in serious life-changing injuries or fatalities. Whilst I have explained the regulations and the risk management steps that should be in place for various activities and locations, unfortunately we still live in a world of complacency and cutting corners. There are also accidents that could not have been prevented no matter what risk controls were put in place. HSE investigations will determine whether the company was at fault in any way, or whether they had taken all reasonable and possible precautions.

Just one final point, on what insurers like to see in their potential clients - accreditations, particularly some key ones noted throughout the book. Some accreditations don't represent quality or safety, but are more like membership of a club. However there are a number of prestigious accreditations (such as NASC) that represent full compliance with Regulations, high standards of workmanship, and meticulous Health and Safety procedures. This will also be reflected in their claims experience - they haven't just been lucky, they have been proactive in creating, implementing and continuously reviewing their risk management processes.

# References

**Websites**

Health & Safety Executive - www.hse.gov.uk

Fire Protection Association - www.thefpa.co.uk

Control of Substances Hazardous to Health (COSHH) - www.hse.gov.uk/coshh/

The Joint Contracts Tribunal - jctltd.co.uk

Construction Industry Training Board (CITB) - CITB.co.uk

Specialty Equipment Market Association (SEMA) - sema.org.uk

Electrical Contractors Association (ECA) - www.eca.co.uk

The Fire and Security Association (FSA) - www.eca.co.uk/join-us/fsa

The Scottish Electrical Contractors Association (SELECT) - www.select.org.uk

National Inspection Council for Electrical Installation Contracting (NICEIC) - www.niceic.com

National Access & Scaffolding Confederation (NASC) - nasc.org.uk

SmartWater - www.shop.smartwater.com/

Heras - www.heras-mobile.co.uk/


**Publications**

Construction (Design and Management) Regulations 2015 (CDM) - https://www.hse.gov.uk/construction/cdm/2015/index.htm

Street Works UK Ltd - http://streetworks.org.uk/resources/publications - 'Guidelines on the positioning and colour coding of underground utilities'

Confined Spaces Regulations 1997 -
https://www.legislation.gov.uk/uksi/1997/1713

Management of Health and Safety at Work Regulations 1999 -
https://www.legislation.gov.uk/uksi/1999/3242/contents

Taylor & Francis - study on weather conditions -
https://www.tandfonline.com/doi/full/10.1080/01446193.2018.147
8109

Printed in Great Britain
by Amazon